ALSO BY DAPHNE OZ

THE HAPPY COOK
RELISH
THE DORM ROOM DIET PLANNER
THE DORM ROOM DIET

EAT YOUR HEART OUT

all-fun, no-fuss food
to celebrate eating clean

DAPHNE OZ

WM
WILLIAM MORROW
An Imprint of HarperCollinsPublishers

FOR MY CHILDREN, WHO FILL
MY LIFE UP TO THE TIPPY TOP
WITH SO MUCH DELICIOUSNESS.
I LOVE YOU ALWAYS!

CONTENTS

INTRODUCTION   1

BREAKFAST AND BRUNCH   13

SMOOTHIES, JUICES, AND MILKS   49

SALADS AND OTHER CRUNCHY GREEN THINGS   65

SOUPS AND SOMETHING LIKE SANDWICHES   93

THE MAIN EVENT   133

ON THE SIDE   183

SNACKS AND SAVORY BITES   217

FLAVOR BOOSTERS   241

SALAD DRESSINGS   263

SWEET NOTHINGS   283

ACKNOWLEDGMENTS   315

UNIVERSAL CONVERSION CHART   319

INDEX   321

INTRODUCTION

I LOVE FOOD.

Not in the abstract, "Oh sure, I could eat" kind of way. I love food in the deeply personal, memory-making, sensory-awakening kind of way. Cooking and eating together with my favorite people is not just my jam. It's my homemade sourdough and hand-churned, extra-salty butter, too.

If you know me from television, social media, or my other cookbooks, then you know I'm the kind of girl who really loves a great many things about good food. I love bright, crisp salads drinking up tangy shallot vinaigrette. I love caramelized roasted veggies adorned with herbs and seeds. I love rich, fatty steaks, salty and burnt at the edges. I love pasta, blessed with sun-sweetened tomatoes and savory garlic. I love fried chicken and fresh fish, simple and grilled with golden olive oil and a squeeze of lemon. I *love* good bread—bad bread is an abomination. And I love dessert. OMG do I love dessert.

My all-time favorite meals have been eaten on paper plates . . . or perhaps no plates at all. Picnics while traveling in new lands cannot be beat. Fresh, flavorful food tops fussiness for me one hundred out of one hundred times, but every great bite is a chance to educate myself and my palate. I like simple, traditional food. I like food fusion. I like familiar comfort and exotic exploration. I'll try just about anything once. Because for me, great meals are life-affirming moments to be collected and savored—especially when a few good, simple ingredients are all you need to get just that.

So yes, food is pure pleasure for me. It lets me engage with the world in a real, adventurous, delicious way I crave. But it's obviously also fuel. I need energy to keep up with my kids—and my husband, and work, and friends, and everything else on my plate! I want to celebrate at every meal and feel good in my skin, too—so my clothes fit well and it's easy to get dressed in the morning, but also so I take on my day feeling confident and strong. And I think it almost goes without saying: I don't really do the whole deprivation thing. I know from experience that when we focus on how *not to eat*, we miss the mark—for health and for happiness. For myself and for anyone reading this book, I want to make it easier to know how *to eat*—and to enjoy it all!

If the point of being healthy is to look as good on the outside as you feel on the inside, then I'd say it's paramount that happy eating stays front and center. These pages are filled with food that nourishes and heals as it delights. Recipes that keep things simple and special. Rules of the road that rely on intuition—what makes sense and feels good long-term—not guesswork and gimmicks. Because if you're anything like me, your plate is already full, and figuring out how to eat and live well is on a long list of daily to-dos. So let's make it easy.

My goal with this book is to share how I cook and eat—with glee and gusto and fun—and still take good care of myself and my family.

Because food and wellness are central to how I enjoy my life, you might be wondering how I juggle this passion for the sensorial delight of yummy bites with the obvious fact that not all delicious foods are "good" for you. How could I commit to—and write a book about—a way of eating that is in some ways restrictive and still feel like I get to enjoy the eating experiences that are important to me? This book is about sharing with you the strategies, the recipes, and above all, the mindset that lets me keep everything I love on the menu. Because people who live for the perfect bite need rules of the road, too—so that when we enjoy, we can enjoy deeply, never feel deprived, and find a happy, healthy balance that works.

Allow me to explain.

My day job guarantees I will never be at a loss for delicious ways to indulge. Cooking and eating together as a family is my favorite activity, but with four wildly wonderful (and wonderfully wild!) children always on the go, there has been much more speed-eating and picking at the kids' leftovers than I would care to admit. Combine back-to-back pregnancies, long days on set surrounded by perfect bites and easy treats at every turn, and my general willingness to make cookie dough at pretty much any hour of the day, and you won't be surprised to learn I wasn't looking or feeling my best. Whenever I would try to rein it in, to regain some balance so that my indulging could feel like a choice that was special and meaningful instead of constant, the pendulum swing to "clean eating only" felt punitive, all consuming, and, well, hard! Did it have to be this hard??

I needed to find a way to maintain my full-time love of food but balance it with a reset now and then in a way that wouldn't disrupt my life, make me feel like I was missing out, or take the pleasure out of my meals.

I have always believed that food can and should be medicine, both physical and emotional. Great food feeds our bodies and our souls. I am not a nutritionist, but I have studied nutrition extensively and am a certified holistic health counselor and natural foods chef. More than relying on calories or grams of fat or carbohydrates alone to guide me, I pay close attention to the results of what I eat. How are my clothes fitting? How are my energy levels? How's my digestion? How's my skin? How's my attitude? If I regularly have energy to work out, am sleeping enough, prioritizing fun and connection; if I'm proactively listening to my body and working smarter not harder; if I am comfortable and confident in my skin ... this is what living well *feels* like. That is what I'm aiming for.

For the most part, I like healthy food with indulgent twists or comfort classics made a bit lighter. That's how I enjoy eating. That's my maintenance strategy. Over the years and out of personal necessity, I have become versed in the art of nourishing Rubenesque honeys who love to cook, love to eat, and would love to be able to breathe a little easier in their jeans. If you're looking for a killer recipe for lightened-up turkey meatloaf with hoisin glaze or oatmeal coconut chocolate chip cookies, allow me to humbly recommend my last two books, *The Happy Cook* and *Relish*, where I shared my favorite recipes for celebrating a healthy balance at every meal.

But in order to press the reset button in those periods of my life when I felt overwhelmed and in need of an extra boost—so I could truly savor my meals long-term and still feel strong and happy in my skin day in and day out—I adopted a simple strategy. It's nothing revolutionary, but it's simple enough to stick with (even for me!), and it really works.

In reset mode, I eat whatever I please two days a week—usually on the weekends. And during the other five days, I eat clean using the following easy-to-remember rules: No gluten. No refined sugar. Limited dairy (choosing goat and sheep milk products). Simple. Oh, there's just one more thing: it still has to be delicious.

Whether you're looking to lose weight, reestablish healthy habits (or break bad ones), or just free up a little headspace that can get bogged down with constant negative self-talk, self-defeating patterns, and food fear that has no business being in your crazily delicious life, this is a formula that works.

My biggest realization was that *a few very simple rules are the keys to intuitive, relaxed, clean eating and ultimate, long-term success.* I needed a strategy for when I wanted to lose a few pounds or break any dependency I was feeling (on gluten, on sugar, and so on), one that could be as straightforward and enjoyable as the way I like to eat the rest of the time. I was looking for a guidebook that would be filled with sumptuously clean recipes I could count on to satisfy these same demanding taste buds of mine while helping me achieve my goals—and not make the process a second, third, or fourth job I *really* didn't need. And since I couldn't find that book on any shelf, I decided to write it.

WHAT I LEARNED ALONG THE WAY

Once it's not a stressful, complicated decision every time you're trying to figure out what to eat, you can finally relax and enjoy yourself on your lighter days as much as you do on your indulgent ones. Keeping it simple and enjoyable not only keeps you confident that you know *how* to make good choices, it makes you *want* to make them—which is the most likely way that you'll actually follow through.

Primarily, I've based the simple "food rules" in this book on what I've done to achieve the easiest, most sustainable weight loss in my body. This is how I eat when I need to get back to an equilibrium where my body feels best, whether that's after pregnancy, after a few weeks with too much stress or too much fun, after vacation, or just generally to reset. I also want everything in this book to be something you can sink your teeth into and deeply enjoy without ever feeling guilty or like you're sacrificing. I want to show the abundance of foods that truly free the eater by making healthy meals easy, fulfilling, and obvious. And ultimately, the food in this book is delicious, so it doesn't really matter that it's healthy. You win either way!

WHEN DO YOU USE THIS PLAN?

I use this plan five days a week, for as long or as little time as I like, whenever I need to reboot good habits and rebalance my body. This book features many of the meals I ate to lose—healthfully, at my own pace—the fifty pounds I gained while pregnant with my fourth baby, Gigi, and I've found them equally valuable since then when I've been thrown off course by too much stress or too much celebrating or just letting bad routines take hold.

I usually follow this plan on the weekdays and use the weekends as a time to indulge a bit more. That's often when we linger over meals as a family or have friends over, and I love being able to luxuriate in these moments and then jump right back on my plan on Monday. The beauty of this system is it's totally sustainable and keeps the pleasure of eating delicious food front and center even while prioritizing your health.

OKAY, SO TELL ME THE RULES AGAIN?

- **NO GLUTEN.** I really love bread, so skipping gluten is not my favorite part of this equation. But I have to admit, when I remove it from my days, my thinking is clearer, my digestion is better and bloating disappears, my skin glows more readily, my mood is more regulated, and I sleep better. And—likely because it makes it that much easier not to be tempted by the many delicious foods that contain gluten (bread, cake, baked goods, burritos, and so on)—removing gluten from my eating to make room for more nutrient-dense, filling, and protein- and fiber-rich foods is one of the most effective ways I see results in terms of fat loss and lean muscle build. With the exception of some gluten-free breads I'll use for fast, open-faced sandwiches in a pinch, when following this plan, I steer clear of baked goods and other processed items that are gluten-free but still not exactly healthy. In general, avoiding processed, packaged foods is my goal. (I include a few of my favorite bread alternatives in this book—check out the Soups and Something Like Sandwiches chapter!)

- **NO *REFINED* SUGAR.** In other words, I still eat fruit, but I skip the sugar packets. Although I use honey and maple syrup all the time in my regular cooking and love many of their benefits, I also left them out of this book. When I need to sweeten one of these recipes, I rely primarily on date syrup. I think you'll see why once you've tasted it. It is made from pureed dates—and that's it. You can buy date syrup online or at most health-food stores and supermarkets, but I've also included a recipe to make your own (see page 244). Very occasionally, when a recipe requires a dry sweetener to really nail the mark, I use coconut sugar—an unrefined sweetener made by boiling and dehydrating coconut palm sap.

- **LIMITED DAIRY.** When needed, I use a small amount of goat or sheep milk products, since many people with allergies and inflammation from cow's milk can tolerate these alternative sources well. Eggs don't count here, and I eat them regularly.

- **TAKE THE WEEKEND OFF.** I usually choose to use the weekend, but whatever two days of the week are going to be most impactful for you and help fuel your resolve to eat well the rest of the time, take them! Savor the chance to linger over meals with an extra glass of wine or get your favorite fresh-baked pastry. The goal is living well, and treating yourself is a critical step in the process!

WHY NO GLUTEN?

I remove gluten when following this plan for two reasons. Number one, gluten is a protein that many of us struggle to properly digest or experience some inflammatory response to. The more we can reduce inflammation in the body, the more we promote healthy aging, healthy detoxification, and healthy healing—all of which are helpful for the kind of longevity I'm looking to achieve!

Number two, gluten-rich processed foods (think anything made with all-purpose flour, aka simple carbohydrates) set you up for blood sugar mayhem that can make it very difficult to stick to any healthy eating plan. Here's why.

Carbohydrates come in two forms: simple (sugar) and complex (starches and fiber). With simple carbohydrates, your body can easily and quickly grab hold of the sugar in a food and turn it into glucose for fuel, primarily because there aren't a lot of other nutrients getting in the way that your body would need to work through first. When you eat a simple carbohydrate like a bagel or cake, you get an almost immediate blood sugar surge. The problem with this is the vicious cycle such a huge burst of blood sugar creates, where your body then works overtime to try to regulate your levels back to normal, causing something of a compensatory blood sugar crash. Your brain responds to this dip by telling you to eat something that will spike your blood sugar again. This is what creates the constant cravings for more sweets all day if you start your morning with a sugary, white flour muffin. It's also why you might find yourself on a roller coaster of feeling hyper energized and then almost immediately exhausted, over and over. It can make it very hard to feel motivated to make good choices when you're operating from a place of total blood sugar disruption that makes you susceptible to hormonal cravings even more than hunger.

On the other hand, if you opt to fill your days with unprocessed, gluten-free grains, fresh produce, nuts and seeds, and legumes, you're choosing complex carbohydrates. Because your body has to contend with fiber and/or starch in these sources, it can't immediately access those same sugars it is after for energy. The harder your body has to work, the slower the digestion process, and the more slowly sugar is released into the bloodstream. A slower, more level rise and fall of blood sugar throughout the day means fewer hormonal cravings for the foods that take you off course. Moreover, the harder your body is working to earn its nutritional intake, the longer you feel full.

WHY NO REFINED SUGAR?

Refined sugar is empty calories devoid of real nutritional value. See the above discussion about simple carbohydrates and the ways foods rich in refined sugar create a blood sugar spike—and subsequent fall—that leads you to spend your day endlessly hunting for more of the same (usually) highly caloric treats. It's not surprising, therefore, that sugar is one of the most addictive substances on earth. It's delicious, of course, and I make plenty of room for it in indulgences that count—the ones that fuel my resolve to eat well the rest of the time. I'm talking birthday cake or a favorite specialty dessert or gelato on a vacation. But in terms of everyday eating that derails you from achieving your health goals, sugar takes over in the worst way.

WHY LIMIT DAIRY?

I'm not against dairy by any stretch of the imagination. Coffee with clouds of cream is my favorite way to start any day, and crackers and cheese (with a glass of yummy wine) is one of my favorite meals. However, the creamy fat that makes milk and its byproducts so enticing means it is one of the easiest ways for me to densely pack extra calories into my day without even realizing. For this reason, I tend to limit dairy consumption as part of this plan to avoid the temptation, relying mainly on a small amount of yogurt and cheese sourced from goat and sheep milk. Sometimes, success is easier if you nip the gateway temptation in the bud. I'm not allergic to cow's milk, and I love it too much to ever give it up fully, but I avoid this particular dairy as part of my plan primarily to limit inflammation, which paves the way for better digestion and nutrient absorption, glowing skin, and hormone balance. I also happen to find goat and sheep milk dairy products delightfully flavorful, and since many people do not have the same inflammatory response to them that they do to cow's milk, they are an amazing asset when a recipe just needs a bit of real dairy richness.

In terms of replacement options, vegan milks are wonderful, and you will find simple recipes in the pages of this book that use an assortment of oats, nuts, and seeds to create the freshest, creamiest, frothiest plant-based milks around. I also love sheep milk and goat milk dairy products. I find them delightfully salty and creamy, and many people don't have the same inflammatory response to them that they do to cow's milk, so they are an amazing asset to rely on when a recipe really just needs that bit of real dairy richness.

HOW LONG DO I NEED TO FOLLOW THIS PLAN FOR?

After having a baby, I follow this plan until I'm feeling great in my clothes again. (I like this metric better than the scale, but do whatever works best for you!) Sometimes I just want a one-week reset, sometimes a month. I do what feels good! This plan is meant to be sustainable, and the beauty is that you can reference these recipes—which are as clean and light as they are delicious and filling—whenever you want and for as long as you need to achieve your personal goals.

WHY TAKE A COUPLE OF DAYS OFF EACH WEEK?

The intermittent break I take on the weekends is important for two reasons. It's an opportunity to splurge (smartly) that resets my metabolism so it continues to operate at optimum levels rather than grinding to a halt in response to lighter eating. But—very important—it also ensures that my mind never starts down the negative path of feeling deprived. And when it comes to long-term success, your brain is the thing to master. Treating yourself to some favorite bites on your days off will ensure you see eating well the rest of the time as a privilege and not a punishment.

Your brain is your most important ally and most perilous foe on this journey toward sustainable health. If you think eating well has to mean sacrificing the experiences you love most, you will never follow through. If you think you'll never succeed at achieving your goals (health or otherwise) because the rules keep changing and the system sets you up to fail or is too complicated to navigate, you'll never really commit to trying. Ultimately, being healthy has to make you happier than whatever you are "giving up" to get there. So don't think of it as giving anything up. Think of it as getting even more.

This has less to do with losing weight than with gaining food confidence.

WHAT IS FOOD CONFIDENCE?

Food confidence is the knowledge that you know fundamentally how to eat to take good care of yourself. That you have the power to enjoy your food fully, to trust your gut (literally and figuratively), and to be able to break bad habits that encourage you to see food as a crutch or an enemy instead of as a wondrously fueling, exquisitely delicious tool to achieve the happiest, healthiest life you desire.

Now, let's talk taste. This book promises you good food, and that's what you'll get—food that is fun, fresh, delicious. Food that cuts some corners—or maybe some muffin tops—but doesn't squander opportunities for big, bold flavors. You shall have your satisfaction—and your results.

When I need to reset, I pick five days a week and give up gluten. I give up refined sugar. I give up most dairy. And I get back food confidence. I get back easy, intuitive eating. I get back a healthy, happy me. I absolutely freaking love my two days off! And then I get back on board with no guilt attached. I do it for as long or short a time as I need to feel good in my skin. And every time I am blown away by how much my body loves this plan.

It works. You deserve this. Let's get to it.

Daphne

breakfast and brunch

OKAY. HERE WE ARE.

Ready to start the day on the right foot! What do you feel like? Something sweet? Or is it eggs? Or something quick? Or something carby? Breakfast is where I set my intention for the day. Whether I'm in need of a fast but fueling Power Up Smoothie or have time to enjoy a stack of protein-packed Magic Pancakes or a bowl of velvety sweet Baked Pears with Yogurt and Oats; taking Gingersnap Granola Bars on the go or craving a savory smashup of a perfect, jammy 6-Minute Egg over Greens tossed with Lemony-Anchovy Dressing; or wanting my taste buds to travel by Lightened-Up English Breakfast, this chapter contains many moods of morning meals to satisfy and set us up for success without sacrifice.

MAGIC PANCAKES WITH BANANAS, EGGS, AND YOGURT   17

KABOCHA SQUASH, EGG, AND QUINOA BOWL   18

GINGERSNAP GRANOLA BARS   21

BLUEBERRY OATMEAL BAKE   22

SPICY BROCCOLI AND FETA SCRAMBLE   24

HIDDEN VEGGIE WAFFLES   25

AFFOGATO OATMEAL WITH COFFEE
AND COCONUT CREAM   27

LIGHTENED-UP ENGLISH BREAKFAST   28

SAVORY GRANOLA WITH THYME AND CHILE   31

BANANA PUMPKIN MUFFINS   32

6-MINUTE EGG OVER GREENS WITH
LEMONY-ANCHOVY DRESSING   35

HUMMUS AND ROASTED VEGGIE MORNING BOWL   36

SCANDI-STYLE SALMON TOAST   37

OAT AND ALMOND PIECRUST   40

ASPARAGUS, LEEK, AND HERB QUICHE   42

BAKED PEARS WITH YOGURT AND OATS   45

STRAWBERRIES AND CREAM CHIA SEED PUDDING   46

Magic Pancakes with Bananas, Eggs, and Yogurt

I call these Magic Pancakes because I still cannot believe mixing together banana, eggs, yogurt, and oatmeal can yield such luxurious results. I'll be honest and tell you these pancakes first came about as my desperate attempt to get my kids to like the filling, fibrous goodness that is oatmeal. That used to involve enough honey, butter, and cream to do away with any health value whatsoever . . . not anymore! The kids do demand maple syrup on theirs, but I fell in love with them all on their own and, should you choose to use it, the date syrup has a uniquely adult earthiness to it that hits the spot.

─────────── **MAKES 12 PANCAKES** ───────────

1 very ripe banana

2 cups gluten-free oat flour (see Note)

1 cup gluten-free rolled oats

1 tablespoon baking soda

½ teaspoon sea salt

2 cups goat or sheep milk yogurt

4 large eggs

2 teaspoons pure vanilla extract

2 tablespoons coconut oil, melted, plus more for greasing

Sliced fresh berries, to serve (optional)

Date Syrup (page 244), warmed, to serve (optional)

IN a large bowl, mash the banana, then add the oat flour, oats, baking soda, and salt and stir to combine. In a medium bowl, whisk the yogurt, eggs, vanilla, and the 2 tablespoons coconut oil until smooth. Add the egg mixture to the flour mixture and gently mix until just combined.

HEAT a griddle or nonstick sauté pan over medium heat and grease with 2 teaspoons coconut oil. Pour ¼ cup batter onto the pan (try to pour in one spot for the most circular result) for each pancake, filling the pan with as many as you can while making sure to leave an inch between each so they have room to spread without touching. Cook until golden brown on one side and bubbles begin to form on the top, 2 to 3 minutes. Flip and cook until golden brown on the other side, another 2 minutes. Remove the cooked pancakes and serve topped with fresh fruit and warm Date Syrup, if using. Continue working through the batter to make all the pancakes, greasing with additional coconut oil as necessary. If you're cooking for a crowd, you can keep previous batches warm on a sheet pan in a 200°F oven as you work through the batter, up to 20 minutes but no longer or they risk drying out.

NOTE. If you want to make your own oat flour, simply add the gluten-free rolled oats to a high-speed blender and pulverize until a fine powder forms. Voilà!

Kabocha Squash, Egg, and Quinoa Bowl

When put at the proverbial communal brunch table where everyone orders something for themselves and then there's that thing in the middle to "share," I want the sweet in the center so I can have a taste while I focus my attention on a very filling, very savory offering. This bowl has eggs, quinoa, and caramelized squash to dredge through thick, garlicky Herbed Yogurt Dip. There is also a crunchy seed topping (dukkah) that I predict you will henceforth be using to add a little texture to any salad, or soup, or grain bowl such as this—it's divine.

MAKES 4 SERVINGS

1½ pounds kabocha squash, scrubbed, seeded, and sliced into half-moons

5 tablespoons extra-virgin olive oil

¼ teaspoon crushed red chile flakes (optional)

½ teaspoon ground coriander

Sea salt, to taste

1 cup red quinoa, rinsed

¼ cup thinly sliced scallions, white and light green parts only

One bunch lacinato kale, stemmed and roughly chopped (2½ packed cups)

Freshly cracked black pepper, to taste

4 large eggs

½ cup Herbed Yogurt Dip (page 257)

2 medium radishes, thinly sliced on a mandoline

1 tablespoon Crunchy Dukkah (page 256)

½ cup fresh mint, cilantro, and/ or parsley leaves, torn

Juice from 1 lemon (about 2 tablespoons)

PREHEAT the oven to 400°F. Line a sheet pan with foil.

TOSS the kabocha squash with 2 tablespoons of the olive oil, the chile flakes, and the coriander and season with salt to taste. Place on the sheet pan and roast for 20 to 25 minutes, flipping halfway through, until golden and tender. Set aside to cool slightly.

MEANWHILE, prepare the quinoa according to the package instructions.

HEAT a large nonstick sauté pan over medium-high heat and add 1 tablespoon of the olive oil. Add the scallions and cook until slightly softened, about 2 minutes. Add the kale in batches, tossing until wilted, 4 to 5 minutes. Transfer to a bowl and season with salt and pepper to taste.

ADD the remaining 2 tablespoons olive oil to the same pan over medium-high heat and crack the eggs into it. Cook until the whites have just set but the yolks are still runny, about 4 minutes.

DOLLOP the Herbed Yogurt Dip into four bowls. Portion equal amounts of the quinoa, squash, and kale mixture and add one egg into each bowl. Garnish with the sliced radish, Crunchy Dukkah, fresh herbs, and lemon juice.

Gingersnap Granola Bars

You are in for a treat. Say goodbye to store-bought granola bars that are stale and probably too sweet to really be called anything other than candy. These are loaded with healthy, energy-sustaining, skin-hydrating good-fat goodness with a perfect nutty chew. Gently sweetened with dates and fragrant with warming fall spices, these make the perfect breakfast on the go or quick afternoon pick-me-up. I use a mix of nuts for this bar, but you can definitely streamline and use 2½ cups of any one type.

MAKES 9 BARS

1 cup raw almonds

1 cup raw walnuts

½ cup raw pecans

½ cup raw pepitas

2 tablespoons whole flaxseeds

3 tablespoons almond butter

2 tablespoons Date Syrup (page 244)

2 tablespoons coconut oil

1 large egg plus 1 egg white, lightly beaten

1 teaspoon pure vanilla extract

½ teaspoon sea salt

1 teaspoon ground cinnamon

¼ teaspoon ground allspice

1 tablespoon ground ginger

1 to 2 inches peeled fresh ginger, grated on a Microplane (optional)

PREHEAT the oven to 350°F. Line an 8 x 8-inch baking dish with parchment paper, letting some excess paper hang over two opposite sides to create handles.

COMBINE the almonds, walnuts, and pecans in the bowl of a food processor fitted with the blade attachment. Pulse until finely ground, with some larger pieces, and transfer to a large bowl. Add the pepitas and flaxseeds and stir to combine.

HEAT the almond butter, Date Syrup, and coconut oil in a small saucepan over medium-low heat and stir until smooth and combined. Pour over the nut mixture and toss to coat. Add the eggs, vanilla, salt, cinnamon, allspice, ground ginger, and fresh ginger (if using), and toss again to combine. Press the mixture into the prepared baking dish to form an even layer.

BAKE for 20 to 25 minutes, until golden. Remove from the oven and let cool completely. Lift out of the baking dish and cut evenly into 9 bars. Store for up to 5 days in an airtight container.

Blueberry Oatmeal Bake

This fuss-free, fuel-you-all-day breakfast reminds me of blueberry muffin bread pudding. It packs a hearty helping of oatmeal and toasty spices, bursts of juicy blueberries, and the sneaky addition of protein-packed quinoa. You can scoop it hot out of the oven (I like adding just a splash of Nut Milk and a drizzle of Date Syrup to make it extra sticky and toffee-like), or let it cool and set in the fridge overnight, then cut it into 1-inch slices and press in a greased waffle maker until gently puffed, warmed through, and crisped on the edges.

──────────── **MAKES 6 SERVINGS** ────────────

1 tablespoon coconut oil, plus more for greasing

2 cups gluten-free rolled oats

2 teaspoons ground cinnamon

¼ teaspoon ground nutmeg

1½ teaspoons baking powder

1 teaspoon sea salt

2 cups Nut Milk, using almonds (page 62), plus more for serving

¼ cup Date Syrup (page 244), plus more for serving

1 ripe banana, mashed

2 large eggs

2 teaspoons pure vanilla extract

1 cup cooked quinoa, cooled

1½ cups fresh or frozen blueberries

¼ cup walnuts, toasted and chopped (see Toasting Nuts, Seeds, and Spices, page 199)

PREHEAT the oven to 350°F. Grease a 9 x 5-inch loaf pan with coconut oil and line with parchment paper, letting the paper hang over the longer sides as a handle. Combine the oats, cinnamon, nutmeg, baking powder, and salt in a large bowl. In a medium bowl, whisk the Nut Milk, Date Syrup, banana, eggs, vanilla, and 1 tablespoon coconut oil until smooth. Pour the banana mixture over the oat mixture and stir to combine. Add the quinoa and 1 cup of the blueberries and stir again to combine.

POUR the batter into the loaf pan and top with the walnuts and remaining ½ cup blueberries. Bake for 45 to 50 minutes, until set and golden brown on top. If the top is getting too dark before the loaf is set, simply cover it with some foil.

SCOOP and serve warm with a splash of Nut Milk and drizzle of Date Syrup.

Spicy Broccoli and Feta Scramble

I make a version of this scramble two or three times a week, but my husband, John, now owns this particular combo as one of his signature dishes, and with good reason! It's easy, excellent whether just for us or to feed a crowd, and always, always has people raving. And I love watching him cook! Benefits abound.

Vegetables for breakfast is one way I make sure to get my servings in, and you can toss in whatever leftover veggies or beans you have to bulk this dish up even more. I like to keep the broccoli tender so there is texture to the scramble, while the onions and peppers soften and sweeten as they caramelize and the acidic bite of pepperoncini comes slicing through. Briny olives and a salty, creamy crumble of feta marry the whole happy mess.

———————————— **MAKES 4 SERVINGS** ————————————

1 tablespoon extra-virgin olive oil

½ medium yellow onion, roughly chopped

1 green bell pepper, stemmed, seeded, and roughly chopped

1 teaspoon dried oregano

½ teaspoon garlic salt

½ teaspoon crushed red chile flakes

1½ cups broccoli florets and stems, stems peeled and all roughly chopped

2 to 3 tablespoons thinly sliced pepperoncini

2 to 3 tablespoons chopped kalamata olives

Sea salt and freshly cracked black pepper, to taste

8 large eggs

½ cup crumbled sheep or goat milk feta cheese

HEAT the olive oil in a large nonstick sauté pan over medium-high heat. Add the onion and sauté until translucent, about 4 minutes. Add the bell pepper, oregano, garlic salt, and chile flakes and cook until softened, another 4 minutes, stirring only occasionally to let the veggies caramelize. Add the broccoli and toss to combine, then cook until tender but not soft, 4 more minutes. Add the pepperoncini and olives and toss to combine and warm through. Taste and season with salt and pepper.

IN a medium bowl, whisk the eggs, add the feta, and whisk again. Pour the egg mixture evenly into the pan. Reduce the heat to low and gently scramble using a rubber spatula until soft curds begin to form and the whites turn opaque, 3 to 4 minutes, drawing the vegetables into the curds to distribute and allowing the cheese to warm and soften.

DIVIDE the scramble onto four plates and enjoy!

Hidden Veggie Waffles

File this under "You can put just about anything in a waffle maker and it becomes (even more) delicious." Leftover oatmeal: check. Hash browns: check. Mashed beets and sweet potato: check, check! The best part about these waffles—aside from the whole hidden veggies thing—is they satisfy that sweet fix and carb craving and really fill you up without the typical waffle sugar crash. Dig in!

———— MAKES 4 SERVINGS ————

1 medium red or golden beet (5 ounces), peeled and cut into 1-inch chunks (about ¾ cup)

½ medium sweet potato (5 ounces), peeled and cut into 1-inch chunks (about 1 cup)

1 cup gluten-free oat flour (see Note on page 17)

¾ cup almond flour

1 tablespoon ground flaxseed

1 tablespoon baking powder

½ teaspoon sea salt

2 teaspoons ground cinnamon

¼ cup goat or sheep milk yogurt

2 teaspoons pure vanilla extract

2 tablespoons Date Syrup (page 244), plus ¼ cup warmed for serving

4 large egg whites

2 tablespoons coconut oil, melted, for greasing

PLACE a steamer basket in a large pot. Add 1 to 2 inches of water to the pot (the water should not touch the steamer basket). Cover and bring to a simmer over medium-high heat. Add the beet and sweet potato to the steamer basket, cover, and steam until very tender when pierced with the tip of a knife, 15 to 18 minutes. Transfer the beet and sweet potato to a bowl to cool.

PREHEAT a waffle iron. In a large bowl, whisk the oat flour, almond flour, flaxseed, baking powder, salt, and cinnamon. Set aside.

ADD the cooled sweet potato and beets to the bowl of a food processor fitted with the blade attachment. Blend until smooth. Add the yogurt, ½ cup water, vanilla and 2 tablespoons of the Date Syrup and pulse until smooth and combined.

MAKE a well in the flour mixture and add the beet–sweet potato mixture, stirring gently until just combined.

PLACE the egg whites in the bowl of a stand mixer fitted with the whisk attachment and beat on medium-high speed until stiff peaks form, 3 to 5 minutes. Gently fold the egg whites in until small streaks of white remain, being careful not to deflate them with over-mixing.

USING a heat-resistant brush or dish towel, carefully grease the preheated waffle iron with some of the coconut oil. Fill the waffle iron and cook according to the manufacturer's instructions, until golden and fluffy. Remove and repeat with the remaining batter.

SERVE with a drizzle of Date Syrup.

Affogato Oatmeal with Coffee and Coconut Cream

This is for those max efficiency days when you need your breakfast and your coffee all at once. I also happen to love coffee ice cream, and this recipe has a similar creamy sweetness from the coconut milk, silky oats (the chia seeds add a nice texture), and date syrup—and then of course that welcome jolt of espresso.

MAKES 4 SERVINGS

2 cups gluten-free rolled oats

2 tablespoons ground flaxseed

¼ cup chia seeds

Pinch of sea salt

1 tablespoon pure vanilla extract

4 shots hot espresso

¼ cup Date Syrup (page 244)

¼ cup well-shaken full-fat coconut milk

ADD 4½ cups water, the oats, flaxseed, chia seeds, and salt to a medium saucepan and bring to a simmer over medium heat. Cook until the oats and chia are hydrated and tender, 4 to 5 minutes. If you like a softer, creamier oatmeal, add a splash more water and continue cooking. When the desired texture is reached, remove from the heat and stir in the vanilla, espresso, Date Syrup, and coconut milk. Heat over low heat, stirring frequently, until combined and warmed through. Divide among four bowls and enjoy.

Lightened-Up English Breakfast

There is just something so genius about a one-skillet breakfast with this many flavor combinations—fatty, acidic, earthy, starchy, herby. I lived in London for a summer in college, and the full English breakfast (baked beans, ham, bacon, eggs, fried tomatoes, black pudding, toast, and jam—the list goes on!) became something I savored most weekends. It is also quite possibly the world's best hangover cure—but you already knew that, didn't you.

This is my lightened-up take to make it a little more weekday- and waistline-friendly, but I left just enough of the good stuff to make sure it hits the spot. The sausage adds a layer of indulgence, and its richness flavors the mushrooms and beans, while bright thyme and juicy tomatoes keep everything fresh.

MAKES 4 SERVINGS

2 tablespoons extra-virgin olive oil

2 chicken sausages, split in half lengthwise

1 shallot, finely chopped

10 ounces cremini mushrooms, stems trimmed, caps thinly sliced

2 garlic cloves, minced

One 15-ounce can navy beans, drained and rinsed

Sea salt and freshly cracked black pepper, to taste

½ teaspoon fresh thyme leaves

4 ripe Roma tomatoes, cut in half lengthwise

⅓ cup vegetable stock or water

4 large eggs

HEAT 1½ tablespoons of the olive oil in a large cast-iron skillet over medium heat. Add the chicken sausage, cut side down, and cook until browned on both sides, 4 to 5 minutes total. Remove and set aside. Add the shallot and mushrooms to the same pan and sauté until just beginning to soften, 4 to 5 minutes. Add the garlic, beans, salt, pepper, and thyme. Stir to combine, then push to one side of the skillet to continue to heat through. Add the sausage back on the other side of the skillet to stay warm and add the tomatoes to the center of the pan, cut side down. Let them gently soften and brown, about 4 minutes. Season the whole skillet with salt and pepper.

REMOVE the sausage and tomatoes and distribute among four serving plates, then deglaze the pan with the vegetable stock, using a wooden spoon to scrape up any flavor left on the pan surface, and let simmer until the stock has evaporated. Divide the mushrooms and beans evenly among the serving plates.

ADD the remaining ½ tablespoon olive oil to the skillet and crack in the eggs. Cook until the whites are set but the yolks are still runny, about 4 minutes. Divide the eggs among the plates and dig in.

Savory Granola with Thyme and Chile

This is one of the most bizarrely addictive recipes I have ever made. You look at this granola and you *expect* it to be sweet. Instead, what you get is a gorgeous hit of gentle heat and just enough toasted fresh thyme for an herbaceous crunch that scents the whole mix. I have to tell you, I'm as likely to make a sweet-tart bowl with this granola over yogurt with halved cherries and raspberries as I am to make a savory one over yogurt with chopped cucumbers, a touch of olive oil, and a little extra salt and fresh oregano if I have it. Wildly weird and wonderful. Just like us!

--- MAKES 5 TO 6 CUPS ---

2 tablespoons coconut oil, melted

2 cups gluten-free rolled oats

1 cup sliced almonds

1 cup raw walnuts, roughly chopped

1 cup raw pecans, roughly chopped

⅓ cup hemp hearts

⅓ cup whole flaxseeds

½ cup sunflower seeds

1 tablespoon fresh thyme leaves

1 teaspoon ground coriander

1 teaspoon cumin seeds

½ teaspoon crushed red chile flakes

½ teaspoon sea salt

½ cup golden raisins or chopped dried apricots (optional)

PREHEAT the oven to 325ºF. Line two sheet pans with parchment paper.

IN a large bowl, combine the melted coconut oil, oats, almonds, walnuts, pecans, hemp hearts, flaxseeds, sunflower seeds, thyme, coriander, cumin seeds, chile flakes, and salt and mix to thoroughly coat. Divide between the prepared sheet pans and bake for 25 to 30 minutes, stirring every 10 minutes, until golden and toasted.

REMOVE and let cool completely. Add golden raisins or apricots (if using). Store in an airtight container for up to a week.

Banana Pumpkin Muffins

This recipe is like banana bread and pumpkin pie had a baby. Unsurprisingly, these muffins are amazing warm out of the oven, and kids love them! Especially spread with a little coconut oil and a sprinkle of coconut sugar. They make for great quick breakfasts throughout the week if you prepare a batch on Sunday evening and warm them as needed on a sheet pan in a 300°F oven until heated through, 5 to 10 minutes. Such a comforting, easy, and shockingly nutritious way to start the day, which is more than most muffins can say!

──────────── **MAKES 12 MUFFINS** ────────────

¾ cup almond flour

¾ cup oat flour (see Note on page 17)

1 teaspoon baking soda

1 teaspoon ground cinnamon

½ teaspoon ground cardamom

½ teaspoon sea salt

2 ripe bananas, mashed (about 1 cup)

1 cup canned pumpkin puree

2 large eggs, whisked

2 tablespoons coconut oil, melted

2 tablespoons Date Syrup (page 244)

2 teaspoons pure vanilla extract

¾ cup chopped walnuts

PREHEAT the oven to 350°F. Fill a 12-well muffin tin with liners.

IN a large bowl, whisk the almond flour, oat flour, baking soda, cinnamon, cardamom, and salt.

IN a medium bowl, combine the mashed bananas, pumpkin puree, whisked eggs, coconut oil, Date Syrup, and vanilla. Stir until smooth.

MAKE a well in the flour mixture, add the banana-pumpkin mixture, and mix until just combined. Fold in half of the walnuts.

SCOOP the batter into the muffin liners, filling each about two-thirds full, and sprinkle the remaining walnuts on top.

BAKE for 25 to 30 minutes, until the muffins are golden and an inserted toothpick comes out clean.

LET cool in the pan for 10 minutes, then enjoy warm or transfer the muffins to a wire rack to cool completely. Store in an airtight container at room temperature for up to 4 days or in the freezer for up to 2 months.

6-Minute Egg over Greens with Lemony-Anchovy Dressing

Yes, I know anchovies are highly polarizing and that I'm crazy to suggest them for breakfast, but hear me out. Lemons and anchovies are two exceptional ways to bring tons of flavor and excitement to otherwise sometimes dull tasks . . . like eating all your greens. I am going to convince you that eating kale and spinach and arugula for breakfast is not just palatable but delightful, especially in concert with the jammiest of yolks from easy-to-perfect 6-minute eggs.

You can enjoy this one of two ways: either over raw, massaged greens—leafier, with more live nutrition—or over sautéed ones that are softened but still packed with green vibrance.

───────────────── **MAKES 2 SERVINGS** ─────────────────

4 large eggs

10 ounces baby kale

1 to 2 tablespoons extra-virgin olive oil

4 cups packed baby spinach

¼ cup chopped fresh chives, plus more for garnish

4 cups packed baby arugula

½ cup Lemon Anchovy Dressing (page 281)

Sea salt and freshly cracked black pepper, to taste

Flaky sea salt, to garnish (optional)

Zest from ½ lemon, to serve

PREPARE an ice bath in a medium bowl.

BRING a medium pot of water to a soft boil. Gently add the eggs, bring the water back to a boil, and cook for 6 minutes. Immediately transfer the eggs to the ice bath using a slotted spoon. Let cool until easy to handle but still warm. Carefully remove the shells.

YOU now have a choose-your-own-adventure of whether to enjoy your greens raw or cooked. If eating raw, toss the kale with the olive oil and use your hands to gently crush and pinch the leaves so they soften and turn a vibrant dark green; this will make the kale easier to chew and much more delicious. Mix the massaged kale with fresh spinach, chives, and arugula and move on to the next step. If you are cooking the greens, rather than massage the kale, add 1 tablespoon of olive oil to a large cast-iron skillet and heat until shimmering over high heat. Add in the kale and spinach, working in batches and adding another tablespoon of olive oil as needed, to char the greens, tossing occasionally, 2 to 3 minutes. Transfer the greens to a large bowl, add the chives and the arugula, and toss to combine.

DRIZZLE the massaged or charred greens with Lemon Anchovy Dressing, toss to coat, and season with salt and pepper.

DIVIDE the greens among two plates. Cut each egg in half and place four halves on each plate. Sprinkle with flaky sea salt (if using), lemon zest, and more chives.

Hummus and Roasted Veggie
Morning Bowl

I don't get it, you're thinking. Hummus is a snack! It is, of course. But it's also the protein-packed creamy base for quick sautéed veggies, peppery arugula, a smattering of dukkah, some creamy feta, and bright, fresh Parsley and Mint Gremolata that has the ability to chase away morning hunger and leave you ready to take on the day with easy energy. Spice up your morning and see what happens!

───────────────── **MAKES 4 SERVINGS** ─────────────────

2 tablespoons extra-virgin olive oil

1 medium yellow squash or zucchini, cut into ½-inch dice

1 red bell pepper, seeded and cut into ½-inch chunks

2 carrots, peeled and thinly sliced

1 garlic clove, minced

1 teaspoon cumin seeds

Sea salt and freshly cracked black pepper, to taste

1 cup Green (page 239), Beet (page 238), or Classic Hummus (page 236)

4 cups baby arugula

2 tablespoons Crunchy Dukkah (page 256)

⅓ cup crumbled sheep or goat milk feta cheese

2 tablespoons Parsley and Mint Gremolata (page 255)

HEAT the olive oil in a large sauté pan over medium-high heat. Add the squash, bell pepper, and carrots and cook until softened and lightly browned, 5 to 6 minutes. Add the garlic and cumin seeds, season with salt and pepper, and cook another minute.

DIVIDE the hummus among four bowls. Top each bowl with a quarter of the vegetable mixture, arugula, Crunchy Dukkah, feta, and Parsley and Mint Gremolata.

Scandi-Style Salmon Toast

There's not a lot of bread in this book, but this open-faced, ultra-fast breakfast sandwich is something I do love now and then—especially because my kids love it, too! When it comes to choosing the right bread for toast, I opt for gluten-free with no sugar added and as unprocessed as possible, which is why homemade or local bakery options are so welcome, though there are great commercial varieties available. Explore what's out there and what your body responds to best!

For this recipe, I swap out the usual cream cheese for sliced avocado (which boosts the glossy hair and glowing skin benefits of the salmon) and add pickled red onion, lemon zest, and a little pile of thinly sliced cucumber for some fresh crunch. You can also skip the bread entirely and make this as an easy salmon plate served with some brown rice cakes or the Easy Seeded Cracker Bark (page 231) for a bit of scooping and crunch!

MAKES 2 SERVINGS

2 slices gluten-free bread

½ ripe avocado

Sea salt, to taste

Zest and juice from 1 lemon

½ English cucumber, thinly sliced

4 ounces smoked or roasted salmon

¼ cup Quick-Pickled Onions (page 246)

2 tablespoons capers, drained

¼ cup minced fresh chives

Fresh dill leaves (optional)

Flaky sea salt (optional)

Freshly cracked black pepper, to taste

TOAST the bread until golden. Lightly mash the avocado in a small bowl and add a pinch of salt and the juice from half a lemon. Spread half of the avocado mash on top of each piece of toast and shingle with the cucumber slices. Top with the smoked salmon and pickled onion and sprinkle with the capers, chives, dill (if using), lemon zest, flaky salt (if using), pepper, and a squeeze of the remaining lemon juice.

LOOKING FOR A YUMMY DIY SEEDED BREAD?

If you want to make your own bread to use in this recipe, my friend and food stylist extraordinaire Frances Boswell introduced me to Adventure Bread from San Francisco's The Mill bakery. Grab their cookbook or google the recipe and make a loaf immediately—it is as easy as measuring and having patience. Soon you will be devouring a richly seeded, gluten-free loaf that's amazing for this combo and equally superlative spread with a bit of nut butter, drizzled with date syrup, and sprinkled with sea salt.

Oat and Almond Piecrust

This was the hardest recipe in the book to test and perfect. I wanted it tender, rich, and delicately crisp but not too crumbly. Reminiscent of true quiche crust but somehow healthy enough to find its way here... without the butter or the all-purpose flour. An epic quest! And here she is! I love it for sweet or savory fillings, including the Asparagus, Leek, and Herb Quiche that follows on page 42 and the Red Berry Slab Pie on page 290.

MAKES ONE 9-INCH PIECRUST

1 cup almond flour

2/3 cup tapioca flour

1/3 cup oat flour (see Note on page 17)

Pinch of sea salt

1 tablespoon Date Syrup (page 244), but omit for savory pies

6 tablespoons solid coconut oil, room temperature

1 large egg

IN the bowl of a food processor fitted with the blade attachment, combine the almond flour, tapioca flour, oat flour, and salt and pulse until mixed well. It's important that you use solid but softened coconut oil for this next step. If your coconut oil has turned liquid, chill it in the refrigerator for 15 to 30 minutes until solid, then set out at room temperature for another 15 to 30 minutes until the chill is gone but the oil is still solid before proceeding. Add the Date Syrup (if using) and solid coconut oil to you flour mix and pulse until crumbles begin to form. Add the egg and blend until the ingredients are combined and a ball of dough begins to form. Remove from the food processor and press into a 1-inch-thick flat round.

USE immediately (no refrigeration necessary!) or wrap in plastic wrap and store in the refrigerator for up to 1 week or the freezer for up to 1 month.

GRATE AND PRESS METHOD

WRAP the fresh piecrust round in plastic wrap and freeze it for 20 minutes. (If you're starting from a frozen round, let it sit at room temperature for 30 to 45 minutes, until chilled but slightly soft to the touch.) Grate the chilled crust on the large holes of a box grater. Press three-quarters of the grated piecrust into the bottom of a 9-inch pie plate. Press the crust up the sides of the pie plate, but do not form a lip or fluted edge (this causes the crust to break and sink). Reserve the remaining piecrust for a different use—see Note opposite for suggestions!

ROLL OUT METHOD

USING a rolling pin, roll out the fresh dough between two pieces of parchment paper to ¼ inch thick and about 9½ inches in diameter. (If using frozen dough, let it thaw completely at room temperature, 1½ to 1¾ hours.) Lay the dough in a 9-inch pie plate and press it up the sides (this dough is very forgiving, so it's easy to patch any holes!). Trim the edges and do not form a lip or fluted edge (this causes the crust to break and sink).

ONCE the dough is in the pie dish, if a recipe calls for parbaking or prebaking the crust, preheat the oven to 350°F. Prick the bottom of the piecrust with a fork and place the pie plate on a sheet pan. Bake for 10 to 14 minutes, until just golden. Let cool completely.

IF the recipe does not call for parbaking or prebaking, fill the crust and bake as directed.

NOTE. Got leftover piecrust? Make Cinnamon "Sugar" Pie Strips. Brush date syrup lightly over the piecrust, cut it into 2-inch strips, and sprinkle with cinnamon and a pinch of salt. Bake at 350°F for 10 to 15 minutes, until golden brown. These are fun little sweet pick-me-ups with a mug of tea in the afternoon.

Asparagus, Leek, and Herb Quiche

I will be so proud of you if you attempt this recipe! It is not the easiest. The techniques aren't super challenging, but there are several layers. This is my promise to you: If you make this quiche, it will have been time well spent. Maybe you will become a better cook along the way. Maybe it will be easy for you and act as a sort of meditation. But either way, at the end of it, you will have yourself a vibrantly flavorful, extremely impressive, gluten-free quiche.

MAKES 6 SERVINGS

2 tablespoons extra-virgin olive oil

6 ounces asparagus, trimmed and cut into 1-inch pieces (about 1½ cups)

2 to 3 leeks, cleaned and thinly sliced (about 2 cups)

2 garlic cloves, minced

Sea salt and freshly cracked black pepper, to taste

3 large eggs

½ cup full-fat goat or sheep milk yogurt

¼ cup Nut Milk, using almonds (page 62)

2 teaspoons fresh thyme leaves

⅓ cup chopped fresh parsley leaves and stems

¼ cup chopped fresh chives

3 tablespoons chopped fresh tarragon

1 recipe Oat and Almond Piecrust (page 40), made without Date Syrup, parbaked in a pie plate and cooled

⅓ cup crumbled goat cheese

PREHEAT the oven to 350ºF.

TO make the filling, heat the olive oil in a large sauté pan over medium-high heat. Add the asparagus, leeks, and garlic and sauté until softened, about 4 minutes. Season with salt and pepper. Transfer to a large bowl and let cool to room temperature.

IN a separate large bowl, whisk the eggs, yogurt, and Nut Milk. Add the thyme, parsley, chives, and tarragon and season with ½ teaspoon salt and ¼ teaspoon pepper.

PLACE the pie plate on a sheet pan to prevent spills. Arrange the asparagus mixture in the crust and top gently with the egg mixture. Dollop the goat cheese over the filling. Use foil to delicately cover the edge of the piecrust (crafting!) to prevent it from burning.

BAKE for 40 to 45 minutes, until the filling is just set. Let cool completely. Serve or store in the refrigerator overnight.

Baked Pears with Yogurt and Oats

This is just so good. Roasted pears melt in on themselves, softening and sweetening, and are enhanced by a simple streusel that makes this work both as breakfast and as a light dessert. I love nestling a warm pear into cool yogurt, diving into the sweet-tart, hot-cold contrast of their collective creaminess. Enjoy with abandon!

——————————————————— MAKES 4 SERVINGS ———————————————————

PEARS

2 ripe Bosc pears, cut in half and seeds scooped out

½ cup gluten-free rolled oats

2 tablespoons almond flour

1 tablespoon coconut sugar

½ teaspoon ground cinnamon

¼ teaspoon ground nutmeg

¼ teaspoon sea salt

2 tablespoons cool, solid coconut oil

BOWL

2 cups full-fat goat or sheep milk yogurt

2 cups assorted fresh fruit of your choosing, like chopped melon or berries

PREHEAT the oven to 375ºF. Place the pears cut side up on a sheet pan (you can cut a sliver off the back to make the pears sit flat, if necessary).

IN a medium bowl, combine the oats, almond flour, coconut sugar, cinnamon, nutmeg, and salt. Add the coconut oil and pinch the fat into the mixture until a crumble forms. Sprinkle the crumble over the pears.

BAKE for 35 to 40 minutes, until the pears are tender and the crumble is golden, covering with foil if it begins to get too dark. Remove and keep warm.

DIVIDE the yogurt among four bowls. Top each with half of a baked pear and assorted fresh fruit. Drizzle with any remaining pear juice from the pan and serve.

Strawberries and Cream Chia Seed Pudding

Chia pudding is essentially dessert that has so much fiber and protein we can have it for breakfast. In this recipe, chia seeds bloom overnight in light coconut milk and Nut Milk, yielding a beguilingly smooth pudding with a satisfying pop of texture. Blended with swirls of vanilla-scented fresh strawberry puree, this is the breakfast we deserve.

MAKES 4 SERVINGS

STRAWBERRY PUREE

1 cup hulled fresh strawberries or
1 cup thawed frozen strawberries

1 Medjool date, pitted

2 teaspoons pure vanilla extract

1 vanilla bean, scraped (optional)

¼ teaspoon sea salt

PUDDING

½ cup chia seeds

¾ cup light coconut milk

¾ cup Nut Milk, using almonds (page 62)

½ cup diced hulled fresh strawberries, to garnish

1 cup unsweetened coconut chips or shredded coconut, toasted (see Toasting Shredded Coconut, optional)

TO make the strawberry puree, in a high-speed blender, combine the strawberries, date, vanilla, vanilla bean seeds (if using), and salt and blend until smooth.

IN a medium bowl, combine the strawberry puree, chia seeds, coconut milk, and Nut Milk and mix until combined. Cover and refrigerate for at least 4 hours but preferably overnight, until thickened.

DIVIDE among four bowls and serve garnished with the diced fresh strawberries and coconut, if using.

TOASTING SHREDDED COCONUT

Preheat the oven to 350°F.

Arrange the coconut in a single layer on a sheet pan and toast until richly golden brown, about 8 minutes, tossing once or twice and rotating the pan to achieve even cooking.

Let cool and store up to 3 days in an airtight container at room temperature.

smoothies, juices, and milks

WHEN THERE ISN'T TIME TO SIT AND SAVOR A MEAL,

a filling, flavorful drink is the way to go. Fresh juices and smoothies offer a powerful boost of vibrant, raw nutrition your body can easily access to rev up energy and clean-fuel your day.

This section also includes simple recipes to whip up fresh, frothy, creamy vegan milk from oats, nuts, and/or seeds to enrich your recipes when you're avoiding dairy (or because you prefer the taste . . . or both!). You'll be amazed at how many combinations you can come up with to achieve the fat, flavor, and froth you desire.

For the thickest, creamiest smoothies, use all frozen produce. It concentrates the flavor and helps keep everything nice and frosty. And while frozen fruit is nature's ice cream, add bulk and creaminess to smoothies with less sugar by including frozen cauliflower, spinach, or peeled zucchini. Don't worry, you won't taste a thing! But your body with delight in that extra boost of veg.

MELONBALLER SMOOTHIE WITH CANTALOUPE AND BEE POLLEN 52

BLUE SEAS SMOOTHIE WITH BLUEBERRY AND SPIRULINA 53

CLEAN UP YOUR ACT JUICE WITH APPLE, CELERY, AND CUCUMBER 54

CHAI TURMERIC SMOOTHIE 57

EMERALD EYES JUICE WITH FRESH GREENS AND MINT 58

POWER UP SMOOTHIE WITH PEAR AND PEANUT BUTTER 59

PINK JUICE WITH WATERMELON AND BEET 60

NUT MILK 62

OAT MILK 63

Melonballer Smoothie with Cantaloupe and Bee Pollen

This smoothie is a vibrant, sunny combination of melon to hydrate and reduce bloat, turmeric to help banish inflammation, and bright yellow bee pollen for a little extra B-vitamin energy boost! Bee pollen is a pretty potent supplement, so it's worth talking to your health-care provider if you have any concerns— and be sure to avoid it if you have bee allergies or are pregnant or nursing. Don't worry; this smoothie is just as yummy without it! One more fun fact: In addition to its natural toffee sweetness, the date in this recipe brings iron, fiber, and a variety of minerals like potassium and magnesium that are thought to boost relaxation and muscle recovery . . . how nice!

MAKES 1 SERVING

⅓ cup frozen cantaloupe chunks or other melon

½ cup frozen cauliflower florets

1 teaspoon peeled and grated fresh turmeric

1 tablespoon chia seeds

1 teaspoon bee pollen (optional)

1 Medjool date, pitted

½ cup coconut water

1 scoop unflavored hemp or pea protein powder (optional)

½ to 1 cup ice, as needed

PLACE the frozen cantaloupe and cauliflower, turmeric, chia seeds, bee pollen (if using), date, and coconut water in a high-speed blender. Add the protein powder (if using). Blend until smooth, adding ice and water as desired for consistency, and serve.

NOTE. It's easy to overdo it on liquefied fruit—and you don't want to accidentally dose yourself with a sugar bomb—so I try to keep my juices mostly veggie and my smoothies to, at a maximum, a half cup of fruit. This gives me the flavor I crave without setting me up for a crash.

Blue Seas Smoothie with Blueberry and Spirulina

This one's for the mermaids. Spirulina is a type of algae that not only turns everything it touches a vibrant blue-green, it also offers insane levels of protein, iron, and energizing chlorophyll while protecting your cells with antioxidants and helping your body eliminate heavy metals! Phew. It does taste . . . marine. Which is why I like to combine it with banana, blueberries, and fresh lime juice to make it more delicious, and spinach just to make it extra colorful and really nail that iron quota. One thing to flag: If you have an autoimmune disease or are sensitive to sodium, spirulina may not be a great choice for you. As with any supplement, it's best to check in with your doctor before beginning any new protocol.

MAKES 1 SERVING

½ ripe banana, frozen

½ cup frozen blueberries

½ cup fresh baby spinach

1½ teaspoons whole flaxseeds

½ teaspoon spirulina (optional)

Juice from ½ lime (about 1 tablespoon)

2 tablespoons unsalted cashews or 1 tablespoon cashew butter (optional)

½ cup Nut Milk (page 62)

1 scoop unflavored hemp or pea protein powder (optional)

½ to 1 cup ice, as needed

PLACE the banana, blueberries, spinach, flaxseeds, spirulina (if using), lime juice, cashews (if using), Nut Milk, and ½ cup water in a high-speed blender. Add the protein powder (if using). Blend until smooth, adding the ice and more water as desired for consistency, and serve.

PS. Almost all smoothies make excellent ice pops! Keep them a little on the looser side with a bit of extra water, coconut water, or nut milk, then pour into an ice-pop mold and freeze until set, at least 4 hours or ideally overnight. This is one of my favorite ways to get my kids to enjoy fruits and veggies without being asked twice.

Clean Up Your Act Juice with Apple, Celery, and Cucumber

If you got on the celery juice bandwagon, you know it has been celebrated as an incredible gut healer, as it may help stimulate production of good stomach acid that keeps your digestion on track. It's also a powerful detoxifier and kind of an all-around wonder veg! Combine it with cucumber to hydrate, lemon for immune-boosting and antibacterial vitamin C, and tummy-soothing ginger for a deliciously refreshing quadruple threat.

MAKES 1 SERVING

1 organic lemon

One sweet-tart apple, such as Granny Smith or Honeycrisp, cored and chopped

4 celery stalks

1 English cucumber

1 inch fresh ginger, peeled

USE a paring knife to slice away the outer bright yellow skin of the lemon, leaving as much of the soft, white pith underneath as possible—it does have a slightly bitter taste, but the pith is also where so many of the powerful health-boosting properties of lemons hide out! Place the lemon, apple, celery, cucumber, and ginger in a juicer and process into juice. Serve immediately over ice or chill in the refrigerator.

Chai Turmeric Smoothie

Here's how to get all the satisfaction of a chai tea latte without long lines or sugar crashes. I steep my tea for at least ten minutes to really let the spices bloom and flavor this smoothie. The turmeric adds its wonderful citrusy flavor and bright orange color—make sure you handle it with plastic gloves or on a day you don't care if your fingers are a little orange!—and is a powerful anti-inflammatory, which is great to help you recover after a workout or from any stress or strain on your body.

MAKES 1 SERVING

1 chai tea bag

2 inches fresh turmeric, peeled and thinly sliced, or 1 to 2 teaspoons ground turmeric

½ banana, frozen

¼ cup goat or sheep milk yogurt

1 Medjool date, pitted

1 teaspoon peeled and grated ginger

1 cup ice

1 scoop unflavored hemp or pea protein powder (optional)

BRING ¾ cup water to a simmer in a small saucepan. Remove from the heat and add the chai tea bag and turmeric. Cover and let steep for 10 minutes. Discard the tea bag and let cool to room temperature.

PLACE the chai mixture, banana, yogurt, date, ginger, and ice in a high-speed blender. Add the protein powder (if using). Blend until smooth and serve.

Emerald Eyes Juice with Fresh Greens and Mint

I have a really hard time with juiced kale. I absolutely love it in salads and wraps, massaged to tender, green perfection. And I know how great it is for me! I just don't want to have to drink all that greenness straight up. Enter this juice, which combines wonderfully neutral and hydrating romaine lettuce; plenty of lemon, cucumber, and mint; and a hint of the sweetness of pear. You, too, will be loading up on kale's B-vitamin and mineral goodness without batting an eyelash. Serve over ice for maximum enjoyment.

MAKES 1 SERVING

1 small organic lemon

1 bunch lacinato kale, stemmed

1 head romaine lettuce, cored

1 English cucumber

1 Bartlett pear, cored

¼ cup fresh mint leaves

USE a paring knife to slice away the outer bright yellow skin of the lemon, leaving as much of the soft, white pith underneath as possible—it does have a slightly bitter taste, but the pith is also where so many of the powerful health-boosting properties of lemons hide out! Place the kale, romaine, cucumber, pear, mint, and lemon in a juicer and process into juice. Serve immediately over ice or chill in the refrigerator.

Power Up Smoothie with Pear and Peanut Butter

I am a lover of all things peanut butter, but you could absolutely use another nut butter or even sunflower butter here if you prefer. I have been known to compare this smoothie to the taste of a Butterfinger. That's my story, and I'm sticking to it. It is filled with healthy fats for long-lasting energy and satiety, a little bit of sweetness and creaminess from the pear, spinach you won't even notice, and just enough liquid to keep it from feeling too much like a milkshake (if that's even possible). I think you've found your new favorite.

MAKES 1 SERVING

1 ripe Bartlett pear, cored, cut into 1-inch pieces, and frozen

1 tablespoon all-natural peanut butter

1 cup packed baby spinach

½ cup Nut Milk (page 62)

½ cup coconut water

1 tablespoon whole flaxseeds

1 scoop unflavored hemp or pea protein powder (optional)

½ to 1 cup ice, as needed

COMBINE the pear, peanut butter, spinach, Nut Milk, coconut water, and flaxseeds in a high-speed blender. Add the protein powder (if using). Blend until smooth, adding ice and water as desired for consistency, and serve.

Pink Juice with Watermelon and Beet

This vibrantly pink juice is deeply hydrating and may help boost blood flow and muscle oxygenation to increase performance, stamina, and recovery. Beets are another blood booster used in traditional Chinese medicine to improve circulation and vitality and reduce blood pressure. PS. Mix in ½ cup of coconut water and a pinch of salt for an amazingly delicious recovery drink after a hard workout.

MAKES 1 SERVING

1 organic lemon

2 cups watermelon, including as much of the white rind part as you like, cut into 1-inch cubes

1 beet, peeled

1 English cucumber

USE a paring knife to slice away the outer bright yellow skin of the lemon, leaving as much of the soft, white pith underneath as possible—it does have a slightly bitter taste, but the pith is also where so many of the powerful health-boosting properties of lemons hide out! Place the watermelon, beet, cucumber, and lemon in a juicer and process into juice. Serve immediately over ice or chill in the refrigerator.

Nut Milk

Whether you're looking for a dairy-free milk for cereal, to use in coffee or tea, or to give sweet or savory recipes a rich and creamy result, there's a plant-based milk that's just right.

If you truly want to customize your blend (and avoid any unnecessary stabilizers or preservatives—your body is a temple, after all!), it's easy to squeeze up fresh, dairy-free milks at home. Go walnut-cashew-Brazil nut for lusciously creamy insanity or add pumpkin seeds for a slightly earthier silky mix that packs a powerful mineral boost. I love playing with ratios and blends to discover which I like best for different uses.

MAKES 3½ CUPS

2 cups raw almonds, cashews, walnuts, pecans, Brazil nuts, hazelnuts, pistachios, pumpkin seeds, hemp seeds, sunflower seeds, or a combination (buy blanched nuts if possible, and resist the urge to combine more than 3 nuts/seeds or the flavors can get a little muddy)

3½ cups filtered water

Pinch of sea salt

PLACE the nuts and/or seeds in a medium bowl and cover with cold water by 1 inch. Cover and let soak in the refrigerator overnight. Drain and rinse. Discard the soaking liquid.

ADD the soaked nuts and/or seeds, filtered water, and salt to a high-speed blender and blend until very smooth. Line a fine-mesh sieve with two pieces of cheesecloth and strain the milk, pressing on the pulp to extract any excess liquid.

PLACE the nut milk in an airtight container and refrigerate for up to 4 days, shaking before drinking.

Oat Milk

The oat milk craze is here to stay, and with good reason. I was hesitant at first, but when I saw the way oat milk swirled in my iced coffee and tasted its velvety richness, I was sold. It also froths up nicely if you want to make a drink with foam. And, of course, it is nut-free for those with allergies.

MAKES 4 CUPS

1 cup gluten-free rolled oats

4 to 4½ cups filtered water (use less water if you like your oat milk thicker)

Pinch of sea salt

COMBINE the oats, water, and salt in a pitcher. Let soak for 30 minutes. Pour into a high-speed blender and blend until smooth. Line a fine-mesh sieve with two pieces of cheesecloth and strain the milk.

PLACE the oat milk in an airtight container and refrigerate for up to 5 days, shaking before serving.

salads
and other
crunchy
green
things

IT'S TIME TO RAISE THE (SALAD) BAR.

I don't believe in rabbit food. I believe in garden-fresh goodness that whets your appetite, tantalizes your taste buds, cleanses your system, fuels your energy with live plant power— and can do it all, even on your busiest days. Whether as a fast and filling lunch, or the perfect crisp, refreshing bite to complement a richer main, great salads are essential everyday eating for me. And I think you'll see why.

Make room on your dance card for anything-but-everyday Grilled Chicken Paillard with Greek Salad and just-a-little-bit-fancy Watercress with Apples and Manchego. Summer Market Corn, Cucumber, and Crab Salad comes together fast, while Frisée with Delicata Squash and Green Goddess Dressing is worth waiting on the squash to roast to sweet, tender perfection.

MIDDLE EASTERN EGG SALAD   68

LENTILS WITH PICKLED GRAPES, SCALLIONS, AND CELERY   71

WATERCRESS WITH APPLES AND MANCHEGO   72

FRISÉE WITH DELICATA SQUASH AND
GREEN GODDESS DRESSING   75

SUMMER MARKET CORN, CUCUMBER, AND CRAB SALAD   76

FAUX CHICKPEA "TUNA" SALAD   79

SPINACH AND CRISPY TOFU
WITH CURRIED TAHINI DRESSING   80

CAULIFLOWER TABBOULEH   82

POBLANO CHOPPED CHICKEN SALAD
WITH CREAMY CILANTRO-LIME DRESSING   83

GRILLED CHICKEN PAILLARD WITH GREEK SALAD   84

ASIAN CHOPPED CHICKEN SALAD
WITH SWEET CHILI SOY DRESSING   87

GRILLED RADICCHIO AND PEACH SALAD   88

ENDIVE AND TUNA WITH CASTELVETRANO OLIVES   91

Middle Eastern Egg Salad

A twist on the deli staple, this egg salad trades in cucumber for celery and tahini for mayo, while the jammy eggs are just runny enough to lend a deliciously rich silkiness to the mix. Add a mountain of fresh herbs and you have something sublimely familiar and exotic all at once. I love to scoop little heaps of this up with crisp cucumber slices for extra crunch and hydration, or layer it onto a rib of romaine or other lettuce cup.

——————————————— **MAKES 4 SERVINGS** ———————————————

8 large eggs, room temperature

3 tablespoons tahini

2 teaspoons Dijon mustard

Juice from 1 lemon (about 2 tablespoons)

2 tablespoons extra-virgin olive oil

Sea salt and freshly cracked black pepper, to taste

2 tablespoons finely chopped fresh parsley, plus more for garnish

2 tablespoons finely chopped fresh dill, plus more for garnish

1 tablespoon fresh tarragon leaves, torn, plus more for garnish

1 small shallot, minced

1 English cucumber, half finely chopped, half cut into ½-inch rounds or quartered into spears, to serve

TO make jammy eggs, fill a medium saucepan with water and bring to a boil over high heat. Set up an ice bath next to the stove. Add the eggs to the pan and boil for 6 minutes. Immediately transfer the eggs to the ice bath using a slotted spoon. Let cool to room temperature and gently peel.

IN a large bowl, whisk the tahini, Dijon mustard, lemon juice, and olive oil until smooth. Season with salt and pepper. Add the peeled eggs to the bowl and "chop" them into smaller pieces using two butter knives. Add the parsley, dill, tarragon, and shallot and gently fold to combine (the runny yolks will become part of the sauce). Add the chopped cucumber and season with additional salt and pepper if necessary.

SERVE with cucumber slices or spears for scooping or dipping, or dollop onto the bread or crackers of your choosing.

Lentils with Pickled Grapes, Scallions, and Celery

I do love lentils! They are so filling, packed with protein, and beautifully take on the flavor of this dressing. The longer they marinate, the better! I added Pickled Grapes for a little burst of juicy sweetness and acidity, and the dish is lightened up with celery leaves—often neglected but extremely delicious and flavorful. You will want to put them in just about every salad you make from now on.

The only trick is to make sure you drain the lentils while they are still intact and al dente and dress them while lightly warm to help them drink up the dressing.

MAKES 4 SERVINGS

LENTIL SALAD

1 cup French green lentils, rinsed and picked through for stones

Pickled Grapes (page 246)

½ bunch scallions, thinly sliced on the bias

3 celery stalks, thinly sliced

½ cup celery leaves

Leaves from 1 to 2 heads butter lettuce

DRESSING

1 tablespoon Dijon mustard

3 tablespoons pickling liquid from Pickled Grapes

⅓ cup extra-virgin olive oil

Sea salt and freshly cracked black pepper, to taste

COMBINE the lentils with 2 cups water in a medium saucepan. Bring to a boil over high heat, then reduce to a simmer. Let simmer until the lentils are just tender and not mushy, 20 to 25 minutes. Drain any excess liquid and spread the hot lentils out onto a sheet pan so they don't continue to steam as they cool until just warm.

WHILE the lentils cool, make the dressing. In a medium bowl, whisk the Dijon mustard and reserved pickling liquid (I like to include some of the cumin, mustard, and coriander seeds as well!). While whisking, slowly drizzle in the olive oil until emulsified and smooth. Season with salt and pepper.

COMBINE the lentils, grapes, scallions, celery, and celery leaves in a large bowl. Drizzle the dressing around the rim and gently toss to coat. Season with additional salt and pepper, if necessary. Serve on a bed of the butter lettuce leaves.

Watercress with Apples and Manchego

This salad is so easy, and yet something about it screams hotel living. I guess because watercress feels fancy, and any time thinly shaved, salty-creamy sheep milk Manchego is in a dish, I start fantasizing about sun-dappled vacation afternoons in Spain. And then there's the sweet, crisp apple, plus some shaved fennel to keep this salad expertly crunchy. Be my guest and enjoy, whether you're eating this at your desk or on the back porch—or in sun-dappled Spain!

────────────── **MAKES 4 SERVINGS** ──────────────

1 fennel bulb

1 Honeycrisp apple, halved, cored, and thinly sliced or shaved on a mandoline

5 cups packed watercress (about 4 ounces)

⅓ cup Shallot Vinaigrette (page 280)

½ cup shaved Manchego cheese

Sea salt and freshly cracked black pepper, to taste

REMOVE and reserve the fennel fronds for serving. Core and thinly slice the fennel bulb, or shave on a mandoline.

IN a large bowl, combine the fennel, apple, and watercress. Drizzle the dressing around the rim of the bowl and toss until lightly coated. Divide the salad among four plates and top with the shaved Manchego and reserved fronds. Taste and season with salt and pepper if desired.

Frisée with Delicata Squash and Green Goddess Dressing

This is so my kind of salad. The squash gets sweet in the oven; chile flakes give it a little heat; crispy, spiky frisée sweeps up the cool, creamy Green Goddess Dressing; and Crunchy Dukkah adds flavor and texture and a little polish to this loose and lovely mix. I love to add the Mediterranean Chicken Skewers on top for a little extra protein!

--- MAKES 4 SERVINGS ---

One 1½-pound Delicata squash, sliced in half lengthwise, seeded, and sliced into ½-inch-thick half-moons

2 tablespoons extra-virgin olive oil

½ teaspoon ground cumin

¼ teaspoon crushed red chile flakes

Sea salt and freshly cracked black pepper, to taste

7 cups frisée, cores removed and leaves chopped or torn into bite-size pieces

¼ cup Crunchy Dukkah (page 256)

½ cup crumbled sheep or goat milk feta cheese

½ cup Green Goddess Dressing (page 273)

1 recipe Mediterranean Chicken Skewers (page 186), to serve (optional)

PREHEAT the oven to 425°F. Line a sheet pan with parchment paper.

IN a large bowl, toss the squash with the olive oil, cumin, and chile flakes until lightly coated. Season with salt and spread evenly on the prepared sheet pan. Roast for 20 to 25 minutes, until golden and tender, flipping halfway through.

PLACE the frisée, dukkah, feta, and squash in the bowl and toss to combine. Drizzle the dressing around the rim of the bowl and toss until lightly coated. Lay the chicken skewers on top (if using). Season with salt and pepper as desired and serve.

Summer Market Corn, Cucumber, and Crab Salad

Some things are worth waiting for the right season to enjoy. Corn is one such item. Sweet summer corn, bursting with juicy sun-ripened sugar, is the perfect mate for salty, sea-scented crab. The bright, bold flavor of Citrus Vinaigrette brings out the best in both, and creamy avocado and crisp celery and cucumber ensure it doesn't disappear so fast that you're left wondering whether it was all just a happy dream. Make enough to share. And if you want to skip the crab, this salad is equally gorgeous with grilled chicken breast!

MAKES 4 SERVINGS

1 cup fresh corn kernels (from about 2 ears of corn)

5 ounces baby arugula

2 celery stalks, finely chopped

½ cup torn celery leaves

¼ cup thinly sliced fresh chives

1 English cucumber, sliced lengthwise and cut into ¼-inch-thick half-moons

½ cup Citrus Vinaigrette, made with lemon juice (page 278)

Sea salt and freshly cracked black pepper, to taste

1 avocado, cut into medium dice

1 pound fresh jumbo lump crabmeat, picked through for shells

Lemon wedges, to serve

IN a large bowl, combine the corn, arugula, celery, celery leaves, chives, and cucumber and gently toss. Drizzle the vinaigrette around the rim of the bowl and toss until lightly coated. Season with salt and pepper and sprinkle with the diced avocado. Serve topped with the crabmeat and lemon wedges.

Faux Chickpea "Tuna" Salad

I almost didn't put this recipe in the book, even though it falls squarely into the category of what I want this book to be—a collection of the recipes I rely on throughout the week to take good care of myself. I make it all the time for a fast, filling, and healthy lunch or snack, especially now that I've stopped eating tuna fish (which I love!) more than once a month because of the mercury content. But I worried it was maybe something only I liked . . .

I decided to share a video of me making the recipe one day—and after hundreds of thousands of views and so many messages from those of you who now make it weekly, I feel confident I'm not the only one who loves this yummy mix. Something about the combination of salty olives and capers, fresh dill, and lemon zest gives real tuna a run for its money!

I love it over salad, as an open-faced sandwich with sliced tomatoes and microgreens, or scooped up with Easy Seeded Cracker Bark (page 231)!

MAKES 4 SERVINGS

Two 15-ounce cans chickpeas, drained and rinsed

4 celery stalks, finely chopped

1 shallot or small red onion, finely chopped (about ½ cup)

2 tablespoons finely chopped fresh dill or 1 tablespoon dried dill

¼ cup plan-compliant mayonnaise

1 teaspoon Dijon mustard

½ cup Castelvetrano or kalamata olives, pitted and chopped

2 tablespoons capers, drained

Zest and juice from 1 lemon (about 1 teaspoon zest and 2 tablespoons juice)

Sea salt and freshly cracked black pepper, to taste

IN a large bowl, gently break apart the chickpeas using your fingers or the back of a fork—we're looking to create surface area to drink up the dressing. Add the celery, shallot, dill, mayo, mustard, olives, capers, lemon zest and juice, salt, and pepper and gently fold until combined.

Spinach and Crispy Tofu with Curried Tahini Dressing

Simply put, tossing cubes of firm tofu in rice flour and gently roasting them in the oven creates magic. The resulting crispy, golden-brown nuggets go with just about any sauce—teriyaki, curry, soy, peanut!—in any dish you want to try them in. In this recipe, they lend a little indulgence to this otherwise very light and tender salad of baby spinach and shredded carrots with a creamy turmeric tahini dressing the tofu drinks right up.

MAKES 4 SERVINGS

CRISPY TOFU

One 14-ounce container extra-firm tofu, drained

1/2 cup rice flour

1 teaspoon sea salt

1 teaspoon chipotle chile powder

Pure extra-virgin olive oil spray

SPICY TOASTED SUNFLOWER SEEDS

1/2 cup sunflower seeds

1 tablespoon grapeseed oil

1/4 teaspoon chipotle chile powder

1/4 teaspoon sea salt

SALAD

2 medium carrots, peeled and shredded

6 cups baby spinach

1/2 cup fresh cilantro leaves

1/4 cup Curried Tahini Dressing with Turmeric and Ginger (page 268)

1 avocado, cut into medium dice

Sea salt and freshly cracked black pepper, to taste

PREHEAT the oven to 400°F.

PLACE the tofu on a plate lined with paper towels. Place another paper towel, plate, and a heavy saucepan on top to weigh down the tofu and release any excess liquid for 15 minutes (up to 30 minutes if you have the time!).

MEANWHILE, make the spicy toasted sunflower seeds. Mix the sunflower seeds with the grapeseed oil, chile powder, and salt in a small bowl. Spread the seeds on a sheet pan and roast for 6 to 8 minutes, stirring and rotating halfway through, until lightly browned. Remove and set aside to cool. Leave the oven on and line the sheet pan with parchment paper.

PAT the tofu very dry and cut it into 1/2-inch-thick strips, then cut each strip into 3 squares. Pat the pieces with a paper towel again to remove any remaining liquid.

COMBINE the rice flour, salt, and chile powder in a medium bowl. Spray all sides of the tofu with the olive oil spray to coat nicely. Dredge each piece of tofu thoroughly in the rice flour mixture, shaking off any excess. Place on the prepared sheet pan.

BAKE for 30 minutes, carefully flipping halfway through, until golden brown and crispy on the outside but soft on the inside.

TO assemble, place the carrots, baby spinach, cilantro leaves, and sunflower seeds in a large bowl and toss to combine. Drizzle the dressing around the rim of the bowl and toss until everything is evenly coated. Top with the avocado and crispy tofu cubes. Season with salt and pepper as desired and serve.

Cauliflower Tabbouleh

Traditional tabbouleh recipes can sometimes feel all about the bulgur wheat, where I always wish they were all about the herbs. I love to replace the bulgur with quinoa and riced cauliflower (you can also do one or the other, but I tend to be an "and" kind of person!) because it keeps the whole thing airily tender. The addition of cucumber and kale ribbons brings great texture and greenery, but the mint and parsley really own the show here. *So fresh.*

──────────────────── **MAKES 4 SERVINGS** ────────────────────

SALAD

One 3-pound cauliflower head, cut into florets, or 7 cups fresh or frozen cauliflower rice

2 tablespoons extra-virgin olive oil

Sea salt and freshly cracked black pepper, to taste

3 cups cooked quinoa (from 1 cup dry quinoa)

1 English cucumber, finely chopped

1 bunch lacinato kale, rinsed, dried, stems removed, and leaves sliced into thin ribbons

1 cup finely chopped fresh parsley leaves and stems

¼ cup finely chopped fresh mint leaves

4 scallions, white and light green parts only, thinly sliced

¼ cup sliced almonds (optional)

DRESSING

Juice from 1 lemon (about 2 tablespoons)

2 tablespoons apple cider vinegar

2 teaspoons Date Syrup (page 244, optional)

½ cup extra-virgin olive oil

Sea salt and freshly cracked black pepper, to taste

IF using cauliflower florets, place them in the bowl of a food processor fitted with the blade attachment and pulse until the cauliflower resembles rice.

HEAT a large sauté pan over medium-high heat and add the olive oil. Add the cauliflower rice and sauté until just softened, about 4 minutes. Season with salt, then set aside and let cool to room temperature.

TO make the dressing, in a small bowl, whisk the lemon juice, vinegar, and Date Syrup (if using) until smooth. While whisking, slowly drizzle in the olive oil until emulsified. Season with salt and pepper.

IN a large salad bowl, combine the cooled cauliflower, cooked quinoa, cucumber, kale, parsley, mint, scallions, and almonds (if using) and fold to combine. Drizzle the dressing around the rim of the bowl and toss until thoroughly mixed. Season with salt and pepper as desired. Let the flavors marinate for at least 10 minutes before serving.

Poblano Chopped Chicken Salad with Creamy Cilantro-Lime Dressing

This is the salad I go for when I am *hungry*. The crisp grain-free chicken strips hold on to their crunch and can stand up to the sweetly smoky heat of the charred poblano peppers. And I love iceberg lettuce—it's just so gratifyingly crisp, and it's the perfect carrier for the weight of the chicken, little bits of apple, and crispy pumpkin seeds. Imagine if a wedge salad took a drive through the Southwest . . .

MAKES 4 SERVINGS

2 poblano peppers

1 tablespoon extra-virgin olive oil

½ cup raw pepitas

Sea salt and freshly cracked black pepper, to taste

2 small iceberg lettuce heads, cored and cut into wedges or roughly chopped

1 Honeycrisp apple, peeled, cored, and finely chopped

½ cup Creamy Cilantro-Lime Dressing (page 270)

1 recipe Crispy Chicken Strips with Sweet and Spicy Mustard (page 163), cut into 1-inch pieces (this is a great use for leftover chicken strips)

2 scallions, thinly sliced

¼ cup fresh cilantro leaves

¼ cup Quick-Pickled Onions (page 246)

CAREFULLY char the outside of the poblano peppers, rotating occasionally to char all sides, 10 to 12 minutes total. This can be done over a gas burner on medium-high heat, on the grill over medium-high heat, or under the broiler. Transfer to a heatproof bowl and cover with a piece of plastic wrap to steam the peppers. Let cool to room temperature, 10 to 15 minutes.

MEANWHILE, line a plate with paper towels. Heat a small sauté pan over medium heat and add the olive oil. Add the pepitas, season with salt, and toast until golden brown, 4 to 5 minutes, stirring often. Transfer to the prepared plate and let cool.

PEEL the charred skin from the peppers and discard. Remove the seeds and stems and discard. Slice the peppers in half lengthwise, then chop them roughly and place in a large bowl. Add the lettuce, apple, and pepitas, drizzle the dressing around the rim of the bowl, and toss to combine until lightly coated. Add the chicken and gently toss again.

GARNISH with the scallions, cilantro, and Quick-Pickled Onions. Season with salt and pepper as desired and serve.

Grilled Chicken Paillard with Greek Salad

Greek salad happens to be one of the things I craved most when I was pregnant. It became my passion to develop a homemade version so I could control the quality of the ingredients and perfect the taste for my unique needs (extra herbs and thinly sliced pepperoncini, please!)—and it's safe to say the cravings haven't gone away. The chicken breast gets tenderized in lemon juice and pounded thin so it cooks up fast, and the salad is so crunchy and refreshing! It's the perfect filling but light lunchtime or weeknight meal.

MAKES 4 SERVINGS

GRILLED CHICKEN PAILLARDS

Four 5- to 6-ounce boneless, skinless chicken breasts

2 tablespoons extra-virgin olive oil

Juice from 1 lemon (about 2 tablespoons)

1 teaspoon onion powder

½ teaspoon garlic salt

Freshly cracked black pepper, to taste

GREEK SALAD

1 romaine lettuce head, cored and cut into 1-inch pieces

½ cup fresh parsley leaves

½ small red onion, thinly sliced

¼ cup Greek Dressing (page 276)

¼ cup pitted kalamata olives, halved

¼ cup crumbled sheep or goat milk feta cheese

½ English cucumber, sliced in half lengthwise and cut into ¼-inch-thick half-moons

1 cup cherry tomatoes, halved

¼ cup packed thinly sliced pepperoncini (from 4 peppers)

Sea salt and freshly cracked black pepper, to taste

TO make the grilled chicken paillards, place one chicken breast between two pieces of plastic wrap and pound using the flat side of a meat mallet or a heavy-bottomed pan to ½ inch thick. Transfer to a plate and repeat with the remaining chicken breasts.

COMBINE the chicken, oil, lemon juice, onion powder, garlic salt, and cracked black pepper in a medium bowl. Cover and marinate for at least 10 minutes, or up to 1 hour in the refrigerator.

WHEN ready to grill, preheat the grill to medium-high heat. Remove the chicken from the marinade and grill until charred on one side, 2 to 3 minutes. Flip and let char and cook through on the other side, another 2 to 3 minutes, until a meat thermometer registers 165ºF. Transfer to a plate and keep warm.

TO make the Greek salad, combine the romaine, parsley, and onion in a large serving bowl. Drizzle the dressing around the rim of the bowl and toss to coat evenly. Add the olives, feta, cucumber, cherry tomatoes, and pepperoncini, and gently toss to combine. Pile onto a juicy chicken paillard to serve. Season with additional salt and pepper if desired.

Asian Chopped Chicken Salad with Sweet Chili Soy Dressing

I often find myself trying to re-create favorite restaurant meals or meals that borrow elements of different dishes and put them together. This is one such mashup. I can't resist a crunchy Chinese chicken salad with its mix of cabbage, nuts, mandarins, and crispy wontons. But whenever I've had it, the poached chicken breast always feels a little … lackluster. It's okay, because the spicy mustard dressing makes up for it, but then I got to thinking … what if I used glorious, peanut-scented Thai chicken satay instead? I think you know where I'm going here. It turns out, if you combine that elegantly spiced bird with crisp cabbage and tender cashews in Sweet Chili Soy Dressing, you're left with the happiest mouth on the block.

MAKES 4 SERVINGS

SPICED CASHEWS

½ cup raw cashews

1 tablespoon grapeseed oil

½ teaspoon ground cumin

¼ teaspoon chile powder or pinch of cayenne

¼ teaspoon ground turmeric (optional)

Sea salt, to taste

CHOPPED SALAD

2 cups shredded purple cabbage

5 cups shredded napa cabbage

2 cups trimmed and halved sugar snap peas

4 to 5 scallions, white and light green parts only, thinly sliced on the bias

2 tablespoons toasted sesame seeds (see Toasting Nuts, Seeds, and Spices, page 199)

½ cup Sweet Chili Soy Dressing (page 275)

1 recipe Peanut-Chili Chicken Skewers (page 188), to serve

PREHEAT the oven to 350°F.

TO make the spiced cashews, toss the cashews, grapeseed oil, cumin, chile powder, turmeric (if using), and salt in a medium bowl until evenly coated. Spread on a sheet pan and roast for 8 to 10 minutes, until golden and fragrant, tossing occasionally and rotating the pan halfway through. Let cool, then roughly chop and set aside.

TO make the chopped salad, combine the purple and napa cabbage in a large bowl. Add the sugar snap peas, cashews, scallions, and sesame seeds. Drizzle the dressing around the rim of the bowl and toss until lightly coated.

SERVE with the chicken skewers.

Grilled Radicchio and Peach Salad

This salad looks as beautiful as it tastes. I love to make it when we have family or company coming for dinner because I can pull it off the grill as they arrive and let the flavors meld and the lettuces drink up the vinaigrette as it cools. Clean, crunchy endive meets charred radicchio, heat-sweetened peach (or other stone fruit, or scatter some halved grapes over the salad), achingly salty pecorino, and the tender crunch of hazelnuts. I love to serve it alongside the Barbecue or Mediterranean Chicken Skewers (page 186). *Yum.*

MAKES 4 SERVINGS

2 radicchio heads, quartered

2 ripe peaches, pitted and cut into ½-inch-thick wedges

Sea salt and freshly cracked black pepper, to taste

2 tablespoons extra-virgin olive oil or olive oil spray

2 endive heads, cored and leaves separated

¼ cup shaved Pecorino Romano

2 tablespoons roughly chopped roasted hazelnuts (see Toasting Nuts, Seeds, and Spices, page 199)

⅓ to ½ cup Citrus Vinaigrette (page 278), made with orange juice

PREHEAT a grill or grill pan to medium-high heat. Brush or spray the radicchio quarters and peach wedges with the olive oil and season with salt. Grill until lightly charred on both flat sides, about 2 minutes per side. Let cool slightly. Remove the core from the radicchio quarters and discard. Pull the radicchio leaves apart and place on a platter. Mix in the endive leaves.

TOP the radicchio and endive with the peaches, pecorino, and hazelnuts, and drizzle with the vinaigrette. Season with salt and pepper as desired and serve.

Endive and Tuna with Castelvetrano Olives

My favorite Italian food seems to effortlessly make the simple feel refined and so much better for its simplicity. This salad is no exception. There is nothing particularly special about any of these individual elements, and yet put them all together and they feel layered, balanced, and extraordinarily delicious. I love tuna, but I eat it only once a month, so I will sometimes replace it with a few more cannellini beans (or flaked salmon!) for an equally delicious effect.

MAKES 4 SERVINGS

One 15-ounce can cannellini beans, drained and rinsed

1 fennel bulb, fronds reserved for another use and core discarded, thinly sliced

Three 5-ounce cans water-packed tuna, drained and flaked

2 endive heads, cored and cut into ½-inch-thick slices

½ small red onion, thinly sliced

½ cup fresh basil leaves, torn

¼ cup pitted green Castelvetrano olives, chopped

Sea salt and freshly cracked black pepper, to taste

¼ cup Lemon Anchovy Dressing (page 281)

PLACE the beans in a large bowl and gently crush with a fork; you want them textured and broken apart but not mashed. This helps them drink up the vinaigrette. Add the fennel, tuna, endive, onion, basil, olives, salt, and pepper and toss until gently combined. Drizzle the vinaigrette over the mixture and fold until just incorporated. Marinate for 10 minutes before serving.

NOTE. Carefully use a mandoline for easy, quick, and perfect thin slices of fennel and onion!

soups
and
something
like
sandwiches

IT'S TIME FOR SOME LUNCH STAPLES—WITH A TWIST!

Let's talk sandwiches. Even though there are plenty of breads that technically meet the "rules of engagement" for our plan—no gluten, no refined sugar, and (mostly) no dairy—as much as possible, I try to avoid relying on even these healthy bread options too heavily. Skipping them means I get to enjoy the best of the beautiful reset this book allows.

My hope is that this chapter will tempt you to turn vibrant green collards into the easiest wraps for any filling. I am very, very excited to get to show you how to make the puffiest, crispiest quinoa crust for pizza. You must immediately make the "beefiest" Lentil Black Bean Burger. Sip sultry Creamy Parsnip Soup with Manchego Crisps or freshen up with Cucumber Melon Gazpacho. Feast on Spicy Crunchy Cauliflower Tacos with Ranch Slaw and savor Shrimp Summer Roll Lettuce Cups. Who wants staples when you can have standouts and stars?

EGG AND CHUTNEY CREPES 97

CHICKPEA FLOUR CREPE WRAPS 98

COLLARD GREEN SANDWICH WRAPS 99

RAINBOW COLLARD WRAPS WITH CRISPY TOFU 100

LENTIL BLACK BEAN BURGER WITH VEGAN CHIPOTLE AIOLI 104

SPICY CRUNCHY CAULIFLOWER TACOS WITH RANCH SLAW 107

BARBECUE MUSHROOM TACOS WITH TOMATILLO SALSA 108

CILANTRO-LIME HALIBUT TACOS WITH CRUNCHY CABBAGE SLAW 109

SHRIMP SUMMER ROLL LETTUCE CUPS 110

ROASTED TOMATO PIZZA WITH QUINOA CRUST AND GREMOLATA 113

CAJUN SALMON BURGER 114

CREAMY PARSNIP SOUP WITH MANCHEGO CRISPS 116

CHICKEN SOUP WITH LENTILS 121

LEMONY RED LENTIL AND CARROT SOUP 122

EASY VEGGIE PHO WITH COCONUT BROTH 125

POWER GREENS SOUP WITH CHARRED SCALLIONS 127

QUICK VEGETARIAN BORSCHT WITH LEMON HORSERADISH CREAM 128

CUCUMBER MELON GAZPACHO 131

Egg and Chutney Crepes

Just another chance to wrap up eggs and cheese with a spicy sauce! I could drink this Cilantro-Peanut Chutney like soup—okay, I definitely have. I add the spinach because I'm always looking for ways to get more greens in, but you can leave it out if you want to taste more of the creamy, cheesy eggs and spicy sauce. And, as it's probably obvious to you by now, once I have them made, I put pickled onions on just about everything for a burst of acidic, salty-sweet goodness.

MAKES 8 CREPES

4 tablespoons extra-virgin olive oil

8 large eggs

Sea salt

½ cup shredded Manchego cheese

1 recipe Chickpea Flour Crepe Wraps (page 98)

2 cups packed baby spinach

½ cup Quick-Pickled Onions (page 246)

½ cup Cilantro-Peanut Chutney (page 258)

Freshly cracked black pepper, to taste

HEAT a large nonstick sauté pan over low heat and add 2 tablespoons of the olive oil. In a medium bowl, whisk the eggs and season with salt. Pour the eggs into the pan and use a rubber spatula to gently stir and gather the eggs until soft, loose curds form, about 4 minutes. The eggs should still be a bit wet.

REMOVE from the heat, sprinkle with the Manchego, cover the pan, and set aside to allow the cheese to melt and the eggs to set.

DIVIDE the spinach among the eight wraps. Top each with a portion of cheesy eggs, Quick-Pickled Onions, and a drizzle of the Cilantro-Peanut Chutney. Fold one half of each crepe over the top to enclose the eggs and serve.

Chickpea Flour Crepe Wraps

There are tons of great flourless and cornless tortilla wraps on the market these days. But these chickpea crepes are soft, pliable, and simple to make, easily enveloping any yummy filling and very good for mopping up slightly thicker stews and sauces. (I call them crepes, not tortillas, because they are poured rather than pressed, but regardless, you get something flat and wrap-like!)

MAKES 8 CREPES

1 cup chickpea flour

1 teaspoon sea salt

2 tablespoons extra-virgin olive oil, plus more for greasing

IN a medium bowl, whisk the chickpea flour, 1¼ cups warm water, salt, and 2 tablespoons of the olive oil until smooth. Let rest for 20 minutes.

WHEN ready to cook, heat an 8-inch nonstick sauté pan over medium-low heat. Using a heat-resistant brush (or you can swirl the pan to distribute), grease the pan with 1 teaspoon olive oil. Add a scant ¼ cup of the crepe batter, swirling to evenly coat the pan. Cook until lightly golden on one side, 2 to 3 minutes. Use a spatula to flip the crepe, then cook it another minute. Transfer to a plate and repeat with the remaining batter. Use in place of wraps for any sandwich!

NOTE. For maximum light, springy texture, these crepes should be made as close to when you will enjoy them as possible! But you can make them ahead of time if needed. Simply allow them to cool, then stack them on a plate, layering parchment paper or a paper towel between each crepe. Wrap well with plastic wrap and store in the refrigerator for up to 3 days or in the freezer for up to 2 months.

Collard Green Sandwich Wraps

I tip my hat to whoever first thought of using sturdy greens as tortilla wraps. Follow this easy technique to give yourself pliable, nutrition-packed leaves that make a tidy little breadless burrito to wrap around anything your heart desires. Collards are great for their size and sturdiness, but you can try this with pretty much any large, leafy green!

———— MAKES 1 SERVING ————

2 large collard green leaves, washed, stems removed

BRING a large pot of water to a boil. Prepare an ice bath. Line a sheet pan with clean kitchen towels or paper towels.

DIP the leaves into the boiling water for 30 to 60 seconds to soften. Remove quickly from the boiling water and place in the ice bath. When cool, transfer to the prepared sheet pan and pat dry.

YOU'LL start with a single leaf connected at the top and with the stem removed. Lay that leaf on a work surface, then lay another "head to toe" on top to give you a stronger leaf setup in a roughly rectangle shape. Lay the desired filling in the center of the leaves. Fold the short sides in toward the center, then, holding firmly, roll from the long side nearest you over the filling. Continue rolling to seal the burrito. Serve.

Rainbow Collard Wraps with Crispy Tofu

Oh yes! Talk about eating the rainbow! I use this recipe to clean out my fridge of all the half-eaten bell peppers, quarters of cabbage, pieces of cucumbers, and so on, and I add sprouts whenever I can since they are such mighty little powerhouses of live nutrition for your body. The taste is so fresh as they all crunch together and use their vitamin-loaded, hydrating, colorful powers to elevate some humble (but delicious) crisped tofu. I like to serve the wraps with a variety of dipping sauces—the Carrot-Ginger is a favorite, but Crunchy Peanut (page 274) and Sweet Chili Soy Dressing (page 275) are close seconds!

MAKES 4 WRAPS

CRISPY TOFU

One 14-ounce package extra-firm tofu, drained

1 cup rice flour

Pinch of cayenne pepper

Sea salt, to taste

Pure extra-virgin olive oil spray

RAINBOW WRAP

4 Collard Green Sandwich Wraps (8 leaves total; page 99)

1 cup Beet Hummus (page 238)

1 cup alfalfa sprouts

1 cup shredded purple cabbage

½ English cucumber, cut into matchsticks on a mandoline or shredded in a food processor

1 red bell pepper, seeded and thinly sliced

3 medium carrots, peeled and cut into matchsticks on a mandoline or shredded with a food processor

1 ripe mango, cut into matchsticks

8 fresh cilantro sprigs

¼ cup fresh mint leaves

Sea salt and freshly cracked black pepper, to taste

Juice from 2 limes (about ¼ cup)

1 recipe Carrot-Ginger Dressing (page 269), to serve

PREHEAT the oven to 400ºF. Line a sheet pan with parchment paper.

TO make the crispy tofu, place the tofu on a plate lined with paper towels. Place another paper towel, plate, and a heavy saucepan on top to weigh down the tofu and release any excess liquid for 15 minutes (up to 30 minutes if you have the time!). Cut along the short side of the tofu into eight ½-inch-thick slices. Pat the slices very dry.

IN a large shallow bowl, whisk the rice flour and cayenne. Season with salt. Spray both sides of the tofu with the olive oil to coat nicely. Dredge all sides of each piece of tofu in the rice flour mixture, shaking off any excess. Place the tofu on the prepared sheet pan.

BAKE for 30 minutes, flipping halfway through, until golden and crispy on the outside but soft on the inside.

LAY two collard leaves "head to toe" so they overlap to make one stronger leaf for rolling. Repeat with the remaining collard leaves to make four wraps total. Spread ¼ cup of the Beet Hummus in the center of each wrap, leaving a 1-inch border on the sides of the wrap. Layer ¼ cup sprouts and ¼ cup purple cabbage on each wrap. Top with the cucumber, bell pepper, carrot, and mango matchsticks. Place a few sprigs of cilantro and mint leaves on each wrap. Season with salt and pepper, drizzle with the lime juice, and top each with 2 pieces of the crispy tofu.

FOLD the short sides of the collard wrap toward the center, and then, holding them firmly in place, roll from the long side nearest you over the top of the filling and continue rolling to close up the burrito. Repeat with the remaining wraps. Cut in half at an angle for easy dipping and serve with the Carrot-Ginger Dressing on the side.

Lentil Black Bean Burger with Vegan Chipotle Aioli

Now we're talking! This black bean burger is beefy... meaty... and totally vegetarian.

I grew up eating versions of these that my mom (who hasn't eaten meat for more than forty years) would make for us, and I'll be honest—even though I eat everything and love an amazing burger when it's going to count—this is the kind of meal I could devour a couple of times a week and feel good about.

I love that the beans are smooth enough to hold the patty together, but the lentils keep the texture game on, and the peppers and onion ensure the whole mix stays juicy. You can absolutely serve it in a collard wrap, sandwiched between a few thick leaves of iceberg (my personal favorite), or on its own with some ripe tomato, pickles (or pickled onions!), and a special sauce of your choosing—I happen to love the sweet, smoky heat of the Vegan Chipotle Aioli both in the burger mix and as a topping. And of course ketchup (no sugar added) and mustard, because what's a burger without her best friends, anyway?

—— **MAKES 6 SERVINGS** ——

LENTIL BLACK BEAN PATTY

3 tablespoons extra-virgin olive oil

1 cup finely chopped red onion

2 garlic cloves, minced

1 jalapeño, seeded and minced

3/4 cup finely chopped seeded green bell pepper

1 1/2 teaspoons ground cumin

1 teaspoon chili powder

1/2 teaspoon smoked paprika

1/2 cup French green lentils, rinsed and picked over for stones

One 15-ounce can black beans, drained and rinsed

1/2 cup oat flour (see Note on page 17) or almond flour

1 large egg, whisked

1 rounded tablespoon Vegan Chipotle Aioli (page 250)

3/4 teaspoon sea salt

1/2 teaspoon freshly cracked black pepper

BURGER

4 Collard Green Sandwich Wraps (8 leaves total; page 99) or 8 large iceberg lettuce leaves

1/4 cup Vegan Chipotle Aioli (page 250)

1 large ripe tomato, cored and cut into 6 slices

2 cups shredded iceberg lettuce

PREHEAT the oven to 325°F.

HEAT a small sauté pan over medium-high heat and add 1 tablespoon of the olive oil. Add the onion, garlic, jalapeño, and bell pepper and cook until softened, about 4 minutes. Add the cumin, chili powder, and smoked paprika and cook another minute. Remove from the heat and let cool completely. Pat the mixture dry with paper towels to remove excess moisture.

MEANWHILE, combine the lentils and 1½ cups water in a small saucepan and bring to a boil over medium-high heat. Reduce the heat to a simmer and cook until just tender, about 15 minutes. Drain and rinse under cold water until the lentils reach room temperature. Pat dry using paper towels.

WHILE the lentils are cooking, spread the beans on a sheet pan and bake for 10 to 12 minutes to allow them to slightly dry out. This helps the burgers hold together and the beans to drink up the sauce.

PLACE the black beans in a large bowl. Use the back of two forks to gently mash them so some texture remains and some parts are smooth. Stir in the lentils, cooled onion mixture, oat flour, egg, Vegan Chipotle Aioli, salt, and pepper. Divide into six ¾-inch-thick patties, about a ½ cup each. Cover and refrigerate for 30 minutes to give the flavors time to meld and help the patties bind together.

TO COOK THE BURGERS, YOU HAVE A FEW OPTIONS:

- You can spray them with olive oil cooking spray and bake on a parchment-lined sheet pan at 375ºF for 12 minutes, flip, then bake another 8 minutes.
- You can grill them on a greased piece of foil, 8 to 10 minutes per side.
- You can heat the remaining 2 tablespoons olive oil in a large sauté pan over medium heat and cook the burgers until golden brown and cooked through, about 3 minutes per side.

SERVE with a slick of Vegan Chipotle Aioli and other plan-friendly burger accoutrements of your choosing tucked into collard wraps (see page 99 for rolling technique) or simply between a few sturdy leaves of iceberg for a wonderful refreshing crunch!

Spicy Crunchy Cauliflower Tacos with Ranch Slaw

I dream about this dish. I want to eat spicy, crunchy Buffalo cauliflower topped with creamy goat milk Ranch Slaw all the time. And, well, I kind of do. I predict a regular rotation in your future.

Humble hunks of cruciferous veggies get tossed in rice flour and baked to light, crisp, extremely poppable perfection. And that's before they get bathed in a bit of your favorite hot sauce—I'm a heat freak and there are a bounty of delicious options on the market today that avoid gluten and refined sugar. A word of caution: You absolutely must make double the cauliflower! Trust me, the first batch always wanders off before you're even ready to serve.

MAKES 4 SERVINGS

RANCH SLAW

2 cups thinly sliced green cabbage

¼ cup chopped fresh cilantro leaves

3 scallions, thinly sliced

¼ cup plus 1 tablespoon Tangy Ranch Dressing (page 280)

BUFFALO CAULIFLOWER

1 cup rice flour

½ cup goat or sheep milk yogurt

1 teaspoon paprika

1 teaspoon garlic powder

¼ to ½ cup gluten-free and refined sugar–free hot sauce, depending on how spicy you like it

Sea salt, to taste

One 2-pound cauliflower head, cut into small florets (about 6 cups)

8 Chickpea Flour Crepe Wraps (page 98) or 8 large Bibb or butter lettuce leaves

PREHEAT the oven to 450°F. Line a sheet pan with parchment paper.

TO make the ranch slaw, toss the cabbage, cilantro, scallions, and Tangy Ranch Dressing in a large bowl until evenly coated. Set aside to marinate.

TO make the buffalo cauliflower, whisk together the rice flour, yogurt, paprika, garlic powder, hot sauce, and ¾ cup water in a large bowl until smooth. Season the mixture with salt. Toss the cauliflower florets in the batter to evenly coat. Using a slotted spoon, remove the florets, allowing excess batter to drip off, and spread them on the prepared sheet pan. Roast for 20 to 25 minutes, until golden brown, cooked through, and crunchy.

CHAR the chickpea wraps lightly on both sides. This can be done over a gas burner set to medium heat or on a grill or grill pan over medium-high heat.

DIVIDE the cauliflower among the wraps and top with the slaw. Serve.

Barbecue Mushroom Tacos with Tomatillo Salsa

When I'm trying to eat clean, I do my utmost to have fun with veggies. They're hearty, they come in a variety of flavors, and by nature they're much lighter than any meat alternative. Mushrooms are really handy in this pursuit because they're so meaty, and they work particularly well with the barbecue flavors in this dish. I love shiitake mushrooms because they are mild and tender with a good amount of chew. The Easy Tomatillo Sauce balances out the smoky mushrooms with plenty of tang, and I love topping tacos like these with some kind of crunchy, hydrating veg—cabbage works great here, or thinly sliced bell peppers in a pinch.

MAKES 4 SERVINGS

TACOS

1 recipe Easy Tomatillo Salsa (page 245)

2 cups shredded purple cabbage

8 Chickpea Flour Crepe Wraps (page 98) or 8 large Bibb or butter lettuce leaves

1 avocado, thinly sliced

¼ cup Quick-Pickled Onions (page 246)

1 jalapeño, sliced, to garnish

¼ cup fresh cilantro leaves, to garnish

Lime wedges, to serve

BARBECUE MUSHROOMS

2 teaspoons chili powder

2 teaspoons smoked paprika

1 teaspoon garlic powder

1 teaspoon ground cumin

1 teaspoon sea salt

Pinch of cayenne pepper

18 ounces baby or small shiitake mushrooms, stemmed (or larger shiitakes, stemmed and sliced ½ inch thick!)

2 tablespoons extra-virgin olive oil

Freshly cracked black pepper, to taste

TOSS the Easy Tomatillo Salsa with the purple cabbage in a large bowl and let marinate for at least 15 minutes.

PREHEAT the oven to 425°F. Line two sheet pans with parchment paper.

TO make the barbecue mushrooms, combine the chili powder, smoked paprika, garlic powder, cumin, salt, and cayenne in a large bowl and mix to combine. Add the mushrooms and olive oil and toss until evenly coated. Spread evenly onto the prepared sheet pans (this may need to be done in batches).

ROAST for 10 minutes, flipping the mushrooms halfway through, until golden brown and tender. Season with pepper and keep warm.

TO serve, char the chickpea wraps lightly on both sides. This can be done over a gas burner set to medium heat or on a grill or grill pan over medium-high heat. Divide the mushrooms evenly among the wraps and top with the cabbage, avocado slices, Quick-Pickled Onions, jalapeño slices, and cilantro leaves. Serve with lime wedges.

Cilantro-Lime Halibut Tacos with Crunchy Cabbage Slaw

Halibut is a wonder in fish tacos because it's mild enough to take on the flavor of all the fun condiments and toppings, but its thick white flesh holds up to cooking. The light brush of mayo (trust me on this one—it brings so much welcome richness!) and lime juice ensures it won't dry out or fall apart on you. I sometimes skip the wraps altogether and just enjoy the fish over a mound of roasted vegetables or shaved cabbage dressed in Creamy Cilantro-Lime Dressing. Light enough for summer, filling enough for fall, easy enough for anytime.

MAKES 4 SERVINGS

CRUNCHY CABBAGE SLAW

2 tablespoons extra-virgin olive oil

Juice from ½ lime (about 1 tablespoon)

½ teaspoon ground cumin

2 tablespoons chopped fresh cilantro

2½ cups thinly sliced purple cabbage

½ jalapeño, thinly sliced

Sea salt and freshly cracked black pepper, to taste

TACOS

1 teaspoon chili powder

½ teaspoon ground cumin

½ teaspoon sea salt

2 tablespoons extra-virgin olive oil

1 tablespoon plan-compliant mayonnaise

1 pound skinless halibut fillet, cut into eight 1-inch-thick strips

Juice from ½ lime

8 Chickpea Flour Crepe Wraps (page 98) or 8 large butter lettuce leaves

½ cup Creamy Cilantro-Lime Dressing (page 270)

Lime wedges, to serve

TO make the crunchy cabbage slaw, whisk the olive oil, lime juice, cumin, and cilantro in a medium bowl. Add the cabbage and jalapeño and toss to coat. Season with salt and pepper. Let marinate for at least 15 minutes.

MEANWHILE, line a plate with paper towels. Combine the chili powder, cumin, and salt in a small bowl. Heat a large cast-iron skillet over medium-high heat and add the oil. Lightly brush all sides of the fish with the mayonnaise, then sprinkle with the chili powder spice mixture. Place the fish in the skillet and cook until it's just opaque and flakes easily with a fork when pressed, 2 to 3 minutes per side. Squeeze the lime juice on top during the last minute of cooking. Transfer to a plate.

CHAR the chickpea wraps lightly on both sides. This can be done over a gas burner set to medium heat or on a grill or grill pan over medium-high heat. Spread a tablespoon of the Cilantro-Lime Dressing on each tortilla. Top each with a piece of fish and some of the cabbage slaw. Serve with lime wedges.

Shrimp Summer Roll Lettuce Cups

I think any meal you eat with your hands feels like a party, but that's especially true when you're noshing on something this colorful, customizable, and lusciously layered. I am a forever fan of the way Thai and Vietnamese cuisines effortlessly marry sweet, savory, salty, and sour together so that your taste buds are always guessing, and you're getting a bit of everything in this neat little package. Tender, mild shrimp. Slippery noodles. Fresh, flavorful herbs and lime. Faintly sweet Crunchy Peanut Dressing. Yum! They also happen to make amazing appetizers, since they're so easy to portion.

— **MAKES 10 ROLLS** —

Sea salt, to taste

1 teaspoon black peppercorns, cracked

Juice from 1 lemon (about 2 tablespoons)

1 pound large shrimp, peeled, deveined, and tails removed

One 12-ounce package kelp noodles or thin shirataki or rice noodles, prepared according to the package instructions

2 medium carrots, peeled and cut into matchsticks or shredded using a food processor

1 recipe Crunchy Peanut Dressing (page 274)

10 butter lettuce leaves

¼ cup fresh mint leaves, torn

¼ cup fresh basil leaves, torn

¼ cup fresh cilantro leaves

¼ cup chopped roasted peanuts

Juice from 2 limes (about ¼ cup)

BRING a medium pot of salted water to a simmer. Add the peppercorns, lemon juice, and squeezed lemon halves. Prepare an ice bath.

PLACE the shrimp in the simmering water and cook until they are opaque, pink, and just cooked through, 2 to 4 minutes. Immediately transfer the shrimp to the ice bath to cool completely. Pat dry.

TOSS the kelp noodles and carrots with the Crunchy Peanut Dressing. Season with salt as desired. I love to serve this disassembled with piles of each ingredient side by side, but to make a beautiful serving platter with individual portions, arrange the butter lettuce leaves on a serving plate and top with the noodle mixture. Top each lettuce cup with shrimp, mint, basil, cilantro, a sprinkle of peanuts, and a squeeze of lime juice.

Roasted Tomato Pizza with Quinoa Crust and Gremolata

I'm saying it now: This is the sleeper hit of the book. Imagine a grain-free version of the fluffiest, lightest focaccia puffy and airy on the inside, golden and crisp on the surface. The roasted tomato topping sweetens up as the fruit bursts and brings a nice hit of acid to the spread of hummus on the crust. A few little pops of toasty pine nuts and fresh Parsley and Mint Gremolata scattered on top and you may forget all about your regular pizza order.

One thing to note: The quinoa does need to soak overnight for best results! And it's worth the wait.

MAKES 4 SERVINGS

QUINOA CRUST

1 cup quinoa

1 teaspoon baking powder

1 teaspoon sea salt

1 tablespoon extra-virgin olive oil

ROASTED TOMATO TOPPING

2 pints cherry tomatoes

2 tablespoons extra-virgin olive oil

Sea salt

1 cup Classic Hummus (page 236)

2 tablespoons toasted pine nuts (see Toasting Nuts, Seeds, and Spices, page 199)

¼ cup Parsley and Mint Gremolata (page 255)

½ teaspoon crushed red chile flakes, to garnish

Freshly cracked black pepper, to taste

COVER the quinoa with water by 1 inch in a large bowl. Soak overnight.

THE next day, set oven racks in the bottom and top positions and set a 12-inch cast-iron skillet on the bottom rack. Preheat the oven to 425°F. Line a sheet pan with parchment paper.

PLACE the tomatoes on the prepared sheet pan and drizzle with the olive oil and a sprinkle of salt. Toss to coat before spreading the tomatoes into an even layer. Set aside.

DRAIN the quinoa and rinse. Place it into the bowl of a food processor fitted with the blade attachment and add ½ cup water, the baking powder, and the salt. Blend until very creamy and smooth, about 2 minutes.

CAREFULLY remove the hot cast-iron skillet from the oven. Add the 1 tablespoon olive oil to the pan and swirl to coat the bottom. Pour in the batter and smooth it with a spatula. Set the pan with the quinoa crust on the bottom oven rack and the tomatoes on the top rack.

BAKE the crust for 15 minutes, then carefully flip it and bake for 7 to 8 minutes more, until golden and crispy. (A flipping tip: Transfer the crust to a plate, cover with another plate, and flip, then slide the crust back into the skillet.) Transfer the crust to a cutting board. Bake the tomatoes for 20 to 25 minutes total, tossing halfway through, until they have burst and have nice color.

SPREAD the Classic Hummus over the crust and top with the roasted tomatoes, toasted pine nuts, Parsley and Mint Gremolata, chile flakes, and pepper. Slice into wedges and serve.

Cajun Salmon Burger

I spent a college summer working a banking job in London where I became familiar with the joy that is excellent fish cakes and tasted just how flaky and moist and full of freshness these little medallions could be (no filler, all flavor!). Those happy memories of cozy dinners tucked into pubs with friends inspired the salmon burger you have before you. But I should warn you—I took some liberties. Okay, a lot of them.

Salmon, it turns out, loves Cajun seasoning, and I went to town and threw in plenty of fresh herbs as well. My favorite way to serve these burgers is over another marine element—frisée lettuce tossed with Lemon Anchovy Dressing.

MAKES 4 SERVINGS

¼ cup extra-virgin olive oil

2 scallions, both light and dark green parts, chopped

1 teaspoon garlic powder

1½ teaspoons sweet paprika

1 teaspoon ground mustard

2 teaspoons dried oregano

1 teaspoon dried thyme

Pinch of cayenne pepper (the spicier the better in this case!)

1½ pounds skinless salmon fillet, cut into 1-inch chunks

2 tablespoons chopped fresh parsley

Juice from ½ lemon (about 1 tablespoon)

½ cup almond flour

¾ teaspoon sea salt, plus more to taste

¼ teaspoon freshly cracked black pepper

2 cups frisée lettuce

¼ cup Lemon Anchovy Dressing (page 281)

½ cup Caper Aioli (page 259)

Quick-Pickled Onions (page 246, optional)

HEAT a small sauté pan over medium-high heat with 2 tablespoons of the olive oil. Add the scallions and sauté until softened, about 4 minutes. Add the garlic powder, paprika, mustard, oregano, thyme, and cayenne and cook another minute. Remove from the heat and set aside to cool completely.

TO the bowl of a food processor fitted with the blade attachment, add the salmon, scallion mixture, parsley, lemon juice, almond flour, salt, and pepper and pulse until just ground and combined. Form into four 1-inch-thick patties.

LINE a plate with paper towels. Heat the remaining 2 tablespoons olive oil in a large cast-iron skillet over medium-high heat. Add the salmon patties and sear until golden brown and cooked through, 3 to 4 minutes per side. Transfer to the prepared plate and sprinkle with salt.

TO serve, toss the frisée lettuce in the Lemon Anchovy Dressing. On each of four plates, arrange the lettuce topped with a salmon burger and a dollop of Caper Aioli and Quick-Pickled Onions (if using).

Creamy Parsnip Soup with Manchego Crisps

This soup brings together sweet parsnips, apples, and yellow onion in a puree that gets lusciously thick with the addition of soaked almonds that have been whirred into creamy clouds, taking this soup to a whole new level of sultry. Also, there's roasted garlic . . . and Manchego Crisps to serve . . . Oh, you fancy, huh? Good, me too.

──────────── MAKES 4 SERVINGS ────────────

½ cup plus 2 tablespoons blanched slivered almonds

1 garlic head, top cut off

4 tablespoons extra-virgin olive oil

1 medium yellow onion, roughly chopped

2 pounds parsnips, peeled and cut into ½-inch pieces

2 Honeycrisp apples, peeled, cored, and roughly chopped

12 fresh thyme sprigs

Sea salt

7 cups (1¾ quarts) vegetable stock

Juice from 1 lemon (about 2 tablespoons)

Freshly cracked black pepper, to taste

Manchego Crisps (see opposite)

COMBINE ½ cup of the almonds and ¼ cup hot water in a medium bowl and let soak at least 4 hours and up to overnight to soften the almonds.

PREHEAT the oven to 350°F.

PLACE the head of garlic in a piece of foil, drizzle with 1 tablespoon of the olive oil, and wrap to enclose the garlic. Place on a sheet pan and bake for 35 to 40 minutes, until golden brown. Let cool until easy to handle and squeeze out half of the roasted garlic cloves, reserving the rest for another use.

WHEN ready to make the almond cream, place the almonds and their soaking liquid in a blender with ⅓ cup hot water and blend until very creamy and smooth (it makes about ¾ cup almond cream).

HEAT a large pot over medium-high heat and add 2 tablespoons of the olive oil. Add the onion and cook until softened, 3 to 4 minutes. Add the parsnips, apple, and 4 of the thyme sprigs, season with salt, and sauté, stirring occasionally, until lightly golden, 5 to 7 minutes. Add the roasted garlic during the last minute of cooking. Add the vegetable stock and bring to a boil. Reduce to a simmer and cook for 15 minutes, until the parsnips are very tender. Remove the thyme sprigs and use an immersion blender to puree the soup, or let cool slightly and puree using a high-speed blender until very smooth, working in batches as needed.

MEANWHILE, line a plate with paper towels. Heat a small sauté pan with the remaining tablespoon of olive oil over medium-low heat. Add the remaining 8 thyme sprigs and the 2 tablespoons slivered almonds and toast until fragrant and golden brown, 3 to 4 minutes, stirring often. Cool completely on the paper towel–lined plate.

STIR ½ cup of the almond cream mixture and the lemon juice into the soup. Season with additional salt and pepper, if necessary. Feel free to add more almond cream or stock to make the soup as creamy as you desire. Serve garnished with the fried thyme sprigs, toasted almonds, and Manchego Crisps.

MANCHEGO CRISPS
MAKES 16 CRISPS

1 cup shredded Manchego cheese

PREHEAT the oven to 350°F. Line a sheet pan with parchment paper.

DROP the shredded cheese by the tablespoon into small piles on the prepared sheet pan. Press down on the cheese to spread it out slightly. Bake for 8 to 10 minutes, until lightly golden and set. Let cool completely until crisp. Enjoy immediately for crispiest results, or store in an airtight container for up to 3 days.

Chicken Soup with Lentils

It's hard to imagine something much more like a hug in food form than a bowl of homemade chicken soup. But when you add faintly sweet parsnips and fennel, plenty of fresh garlic and herbs, and quinoa and lentils to replace the rice and noodles that never did much to fill me up, you're left with a bowl of pure, edible comfort.

MAKES 4 TO 6 SERVINGS

ROASTED CHICKEN

2 bone-in, skin-on chicken breast halves (1½ pounds total)

¾ teaspoon sea salt, plus more to taste

2 tablespoons extra-virgin olive oil

SOUP

2 tablespoons extra-virgin olive oil

1 small yellow onion, finely chopped

2 garlic cloves, minced

3 medium parsnips, peeled and cut into ¼-inch rounds on the bias

1 small fennel head, fronds removed and reserved for serving, sliced into ½-inch pieces

½ teaspoon ground coriander

Sea salt and freshly cracked black pepper, to taste

½ cup French green lentils, rinsed and picked through for stones

½ cup quinoa, rinsed

8 cups (2 quarts) chicken stock, plus more as needed

3 tablespoons chopped fresh dill, to garnish

3 tablespoons chopped fresh parsley leaves, to garnish

3 tablespoons chopped fresh chives, to garnish

PREHEAT the oven to 400°F. Line a sheet pan with foil.

TO make the roasted chicken, season the chicken breasts with the salt on both sides and drizzle with the olive oil. Place on the prepared sheet pan and roast for 30 to 35 minutes, until cooked through and the thickest parts of the breasts register 165°F on a meat thermometer. Let cool until easy to handle. Shred the breast meat with a fork, discarding the skin and bones, and set aside.

TO make the soup, heat a large pot over medium-high heat and add the olive oil. Add the onion, garlic, parsnips, and fennel and sauté until softened and lightly golden, 5 to 6 minutes, stirring occasionally. Add the coriander, season with salt, and toast a minute more. Add the lentils, quinoa, and chicken stock. Bring to a boil and reduce to a simmer. Cook until the veggies are tender and the lentils and quinoa are cooked through, 30 to 35 minutes (add more stock or water if the soup gets too thick). Stir in the shredded chicken. Season with salt and pepper as desired.

SERVE garnished with the reserved fennel fronds, dill, parsley, and chives.

Lemony Red Lentil and Carrot Soup

When I visit my family in Turkey, we eat lentil soups like this all the time: smooth and creamy with plenty of cumin, coriander, and oregano and a generous squeeze of fresh lemon juice to cut through the earthiness of the filling red lentils. In this recipe, I like to leave some of the soup unpureed to maintain a bit of tender texture. A slightly unconventional slick of Chili Sesame Oil to garnish and some Easy Seeded Cracker Bark give you silk and crunch and spice, how nice.

—————————————— **MAKES 4 SERVINGS** ——————————————

2 tablespoons extra-virgin olive oil

1 large yellow onion, finely chopped

6 medium carrots, peeled and cut into 1-inch chunks

4 garlic cloves, minced

2 teaspoons cumin seeds

1 teaspoon ground coriander

1 teaspoon dried oregano

1 teaspoon sea salt, plus more to taste

2 cups red lentils, rinsed and picked through for stones

8 cups (2 quarts) vegetable stock

Juice from 2 lemons (about ¼ cup)

Sea salt and freshly cracked black pepper, to taste

Easy Seeded Cracker Bark (page 231), to serve (optional)

Chili Sesame Oil (page 253), to garnish (optional)

HEAT a large heavy-bottomed pot or Dutch oven over medium-high heat and add the olive oil. Add the onion and carrot and sauté until partially softened, about 4 minutes, stirring occasionally. Add the garlic, cumin seeds, coriander, oregano, and salt and cook an additional minute. Add the lentils, stock, and 1 cup water. Bring to a boil and reduce to a simmer. Let simmer until the lentils are tender, 20 to 25 minutes.

LET cool slightly, then place all the tender vegetable pieces and half of the soup into a high-speed blender and blend until smooth (working in batches if necessary). Return the puree to the soup in the pot and stir in the lemon juice and additional water if the soup is too thick. Season with salt and pepper.

SERVE with Easy Seeded Cracker Bark if wanted and garnish with a drizzle of the Chili Sesame Oil (if using).

Easy Veggie Pho with Coconut Broth

This soup looks complicated, but the process is quite simple—there are just a lot of ingredients, because I want you to have layers and layers of flavors. You can choose to leave some out if you want to do a quick version. But if you do it all—the lemongrass, ginger, peppercorns, garlic, and cinnamon coming together to scent this fragrant broth . . . the little pools of tamari and the sesame oil . . . the floating noodles and fresh herbs—you won't be disappointed.

FYI, unlike traditional pho that often has a long-simmered bone broth as its base, I kept this one on the lighter side by using vegetable broth, but I find it works best when I add back some of the silken texture collagen usually brings with a splash of coconut milk.

──────── **MAKES 4 SERVINGS** ────────

COCONUT BROTH

1 tablespoon coconut oil

1 yellow onion, thinly sliced

2 inches fresh ginger, thinly sliced

2 lemongrass stalks, woody ends removed, beaten roughly with the heel of a knife and cut into 2 or 3 pieces

Sea salt, to taste

1 garlic head, top cut off

1 cinnamon stick

1 teaspoon freshly cracked black pepper

6 cups (1½ quarts) vegetable stock

2 tablespoons tamari or coconut aminos

1 tablespoon toasted sesame oil

1 teaspoon Date Syrup (page 244)

1 cup full-fat coconut milk (light coconut milk will yield a less silky broth but still be richly flavorful)

VEGGIE PHO

One 12-ounce package kelp noodles or rice noodles, prepared according to the package instructions

1 pound shiitake mushrooms, stemmed and thinly sliced

1 cup bean sprouts

2 cups thinly sliced napa cabbage

4 scallions, thinly sliced on the bias

¼ cup fresh mint leaves, to garnish

¼ cup fresh basil leaves, to garnish

¼ cup fresh cilantro leaves, to garnish

1 jalapeño, thinly sliced, to garnish

1 lime, cut into wedges, to serve

(recipe continues)

TO make the coconut broth, heat a large heavy-bottomed pot or Dutch oven over medium-high heat and add the coconut oil. Add the onion, ginger, and lemongrass; season with salt; and cook until softened, 4 to 5 minutes. Add the garlic, cinnamon stick, pepper, vegetable stock, tamari, sesame oil, and Date Syrup and bring to a boil. Reduce the heat and simmer until the stock is concentrated to about 2 cups, 30 to 40 minutes.

STRAIN the stock through a fine-mesh sieve, discarding the aromatics, and stir in 1½ cups water and the coconut milk. Heat until simmering and season with salt.

DIVIDE the noodles, mushrooms, bean sprouts, cabbage, and scallions among four bowls. Ladle in the hot stock and let sit for about 5 minutes to soften the vegetables.

GARNISH with the mint, basil, cilantro, and jalapeño. Serve with the lime wedges.

Power Greens Soup with Charred Scallions

This is a wonderful soup to have when you're craving a big dose of greens and beans. It is extremely nourishing and filling, and I love the taste of charred scallions that gives it a sweet, earthy note throughout. This is the perfect soup to clean out any veggies hanging around your fridge at the end of the week, and it's as delicious at room temperature as it is hot—it would probably even be good cold. I like to leave it nice and chunky (I find soups keep me full longer when I have something to chew on!), but there's also a tip below if you prefer to see all one shade of (pureed) green.

MAKES 4 SERVINGS

¼ cup extra-virgin olive oil

2 leeks, cleaned and thinly sliced

1 fennel head, fronds removed and reserved for serving, cored and roughly chopped

1 broccoli head, cut into bite-size florets

6 garlic cloves, minced

Sea salt, to taste

½ bunch lacinato kale, stemmed and roughly chopped (about 2 packed cups)

½ bunch Swiss chard, stemmed and roughly chopped (about 2 packed cups)

1 fresh bay leaf

One 15-ounce can cannellini beans, drained and rinsed

4 cups (1 quart) vegetable stock or water

1½ bunches scallions, trimmed

1 cup packed baby spinach

Freshly cracked black pepper, to taste

¼ cup full-fat goat or sheep milk yogurt, to serve

Zest from 1 lemon, to serve

HEAT a large heavy-bottomed pot or Dutch oven over medium-high heat and add 2 tablespoons of the olive oil. Add the leeks, fennel, and broccoli and cook until lightly browned, 5 to 6 minutes, stirring occasionally. Add the garlic, cook an additional minute, and season with salt. Add the kale and chard and sauté for another 6 minutes, stirring to help the greens wilt. Season with salt again and add the bay leaf, beans, and vegetable stock. Bring to a simmer and cook until the broccoli and sturdier greens are tender, 15 minutes.

MEANWHILE, char the scallions over a gas burner set to medium heat or on a sheet pan under the broiler. Let cool, chop roughly, and set aside.

ADD the scallions and spinach to the hot soup and stir to combine. Season again with salt and pepper as desired. Serve garnished with a dollop of yogurt, lemon zest, and fennel fronds.

NOTE. If you prefer a smooth soup, cook the veggies as described, then transfer them along with the charred scallions and fresh spinach to a high-speed blender and puree, working in batches as necessary. Garnish as usual for a beautiful, layered finish!

Quick Vegetarian Borscht with Lemon Horseradish Cream

Packed with ruby red beets, cabbage, carrots, and celery and blessed with the sinus-freeing power of horseradish and plenty of dill, this is the perfect soup to pair with roast chicken for warm dinners inside staring out at sparkling winter nights.

MAKES 4 SERVINGS

1 tablespoon extra-virgin olive oil

1 large yellow onion, finely chopped

2 medium beets (about 1 pound), peeled and cut into ½-inch dice

2 medium carrots, peeled and grated on the large holes of a box grater

2 celery stalks, thinly sliced

Sea salt, to taste

4 cups (1 quart) vegetable stock

2 cups thinly sliced green cabbage

Freshly cracked black pepper, to taste

LEMON HORSERADISH CREAM

Zest of ½ lemon (about 1 teaspoon)

1 tablespoon freshly grated horseradish or prepared horseradish

½ cup full-fat sheep milk yogurt

1 tablespoon chopped fresh dill, to garnish

HEAT a large heavy-bottomed pot or Dutch oven over medium-high heat and add the olive oil. Add the onion, beets, carrots, and celery and cook until softened, 4 to 5 minutes, stirring occasionally. Season with salt and add the vegetable stock and 1 cup water. Bring to a boil and reduce to a simmer. Let simmer for 30 to 35 minutes, adding the cabbage during the last 15 minutes of cooking. Season with salt and pepper as desired.

MEANWHILE, make the Lemon Horseradish Cream. Combine the lemon zest, horseradish, yogurt, and dill. Season with salt and pepper to taste.

SERVE the borscht with a dollop of the Dill Horseradish Cream.

Cucumber Melon Gazpacho

My husband and I usually don't agree on a "favorite thing on the menu" at restaurants. And I know he really loves me because he will often order my second favorite thing just so I can try it, even though it's not his first choice. But there is one thing we will always, always agree on and that is gazpacho. We love all the versions: tomato based and full of crisp chopped veggies, creamy with pureed almonds, and this one, which has climbed the charts as our favorite version ever because it's epically cool and refreshing with the cucumber and lemon, but the faint sweet melon lingers and keeps you curious.

MAKES 4 SERVINGS

1 cup blanched almonds

2½ English cucumbers, peeled and roughly chopped, plus ½ cucumber thinly sliced into half-moons for garnish

5 scallions, cut into 1-inch pieces, plus 2 thinly sliced for garnish

1 garlic clove

2 cups roughly chopped honeydew melon or yellow bell pepper (for a more savory result)

Juice from 2 or 3 lemons (about ⅓ cup)

6 tablespoons extra-virgin olive oil, plus more for garnish

1 to 2 tablespoons white wine vinegar or white balsamic vinegar

10 to 12 fresh mint leaves

½ jalapeño, seeds and ribs removed for less heat (optional)

Sea salt, to taste

4 radishes, thinly sliced, to garnish

SOAK the almonds in 1¼ cups hot water for 1 to 2 hours to soften so they will blend into a creamy milk without being chunky.

PLACE the roughly chopped cucumbers, chopped scallions, garlic, almonds and soaking water, melon, lemon juice, olive oil, vinegar, mint, jalapeño (if using), and salt in the jar of a high-speed blender and blend until very smooth, working in batches as needed. Taste and adjust any seasoning.

TRANSFER to a container and refrigerate overnight, 8 to 12 hours, to allow the flavors to meld. This gets your gazpacho to the best consistency and flavor—but if you just cannot wait, it will still be delicious right away! If the soup happens to separate at all, just stir to combine again before serving.

SERVE garnished with the cucumber slices, sliced scallions, radishes, and a drizzle of olive oil.

NOTE. For an ultra-creamy and slightly richer gazpacho, add 1 cup of unsweetened almond milk to the carafe before blending your soaked and drained almonds.

the
main
event

THE KEY TO CREATING DINNERS THAT ARE LIGHT BUT DEEPLY SATISFYING IS LAYERING.

Layering flavors. Layering textures. Tantalizing with contrast and a few surprises along the way, while adding moments of indulgence that elevate the whole dish. The right choices make you forget the simple, obvious, individual ingredients and instead appreciate the whole.

Surprise your taste buds with Lamb Chops with Cilantro-Peanut Chutney and White Beans. Settle in for a slow cook that frees up your hands with Braised Chicken Thighs with Fennel, Lemon, and Dates or Roasted Butternut Squash Pasta Bake. Get a little sweet with your savory with Crispy Tofu with Candied Brussels Sprouts or Barbecue Pulled Chicken on Crispy Smashed Japanese Yams. Even something simple like Feel-Good Turkey Meatloaf has a few tricks up its sleeve. That's why you stick around for the show.

SHEET-PAN TERIYAKI CHICKEN AND GREEN BEANS 136

CHICKPEA CAULIFLOWER COCONUT CURRY 137

SUNFLOWER SEED PESTO PASTA WITH CHARRED ZUCCHINI 139

MAMA'S BBQ CHICKEN 140

SHEET-PAN MISO-GLAZED SEA BASS WITH ROASTED BOK CHOY 143

FEEL-GOOD TURKEY MEATLOAF 144

SOY-GINGER TURKEY MEATBALLS WITH MISO SWEET POTATO NOODLES 147

SICILIAN-ISH BISON MEATBALLS IN TOMATO SAUCE 150

CHIPOTLE CHICKEN MEATBALL BURRITO BOWL 152

CHICKEN AND SCALLION CABBAGE DUMPLINGS 154

CRISPY TOFU WITH CANDIED BRUSSELS SPROUTS 156

SHEET-PAN TANDOORI CHICKEN WITH BROCCOLI 159

BRAISED CHICKEN THIGHS WITH FENNEL, LEMON, AND DATES 160

ROASTED BUTTERNUT SQUASH PASTA BAKE 162

CRISPY CHICKEN STRIPS WITH SWEET AND SPICY MUSTARD 163

BARBECUE PULLED CHICKEN ON CRISPY SMASHED JAPANESE YAMS 165

VEGAN SPAGHETTI SQUASH CARBONARA WITH MUSHROOM BACON 168

DELIVERY CHICKEN WITH BASIL, SNOW PEAS, AND OKRA 171

SPATCHCOCK CHICKEN WITH FIGS AND CELERY ROOT 172

CARROT-GINGER SHRIMP BOWL 175

LAMB CHOPS WITH CILANTRO-PEANUT CHUTNEY AND WHITE BEANS 176

BRANZINO STUFFED WITH RED ONION, LEMON, AND OREGANO 179

SPICY SLOW-COOKER CHICKEN CHILI WITH BLACK-EYED PEAS 180

Sheet-Pan Teriyaki Chicken and Green Beans

Sheet-pan dinners are truly heaven sent, with minimal cleanup, maximum flavor, and the whole meal done at once. This particular combo is always in heavy demand at our home because the kids love the tangy-sweet sauce as much as we do. The chicken is juicy and the green beans are tender and crisp, and you get a few extra minutes back in your day!

--- MAKES 4 SERVINGS ---

TERIYAKI SAUCE

¼ cup tamari or coconut aminos

1 tablespoon rice vinegar

1 tablespoon Date Syrup (page 244)

1 inch fresh ginger, peeled and grated

2 garlic cloves, minced

2 teaspoons tapioca flour

1 tablespoon sesame seeds, plus more for garnish

SHEET-PAN CHICKEN

2 tablespoons grapeseed oil

1 pound boneless, skinless chicken thighs

1½ pounds green beans, ends trimmed

Sea salt, to taste

Lime wedges, to serve

TO make the teriyaki sauce, whisk together ½ cup water, the tamari, rice vinegar, Date Syrup, ginger, and garlic in a small saucepan and bring to a simmer over medium heat. Let simmer for 5 minutes. Meanwhile, whisk the tapioca flour with 2 teaspoons water to make a slurry. Remove the sauce from the heat and whisk in the slurry. Return the sauce to medium heat and simmer for a minute more, until thickened, and stir in 1 tablespoon sesame seeds. Remove from the heat and let cool completely.

PREHEAT the oven to 400°F. Line a sheet pan with foil and brush with 1 tablespoon of the grapeseed oil. Divide the teriyaki sauce in half.

PLACE the chicken on the prepared sheet pan. Brush the first half of the teriyaki sauce on the chicken thighs.

TOSS the green beans with the remaining tablespoon of grapeseed oil in a large bowl and season with salt. Scatter the green beans around the sheet pan, taking care not to overcrowd the pan. Roast for 12 to 15 minutes, until the chicken is cooked through and registers 165°F on a meat thermometer and the green beans are tender but still slightly crunchy. Using a clean brush, glaze the chicken with the remaining sauce.

SERVE the chicken and green beans together, garnished with sesame seeds and lime wedges.

Chickpea Cauliflower Coconut Curry

The best thing about bathing your meat or veg in a saucy coat of luscious coconut milk, spices, and herbs is that you're guaranteed flavor and juiciness. The only problem is that store-bought (and take-out) curries will often pack in the sugar and salt—and preservatives. No need! I love how quickly this earthy combo comes together with toasted spices, dates to sweeten, chickpeas and cauliflower to drink up all that sauce, and a mountain of fresh herbs to garnish effortlessly but gloriously. Oh, and just enough crunchy peanuts (or roasted cashews or almonds if you prefer!) to make sure you're not missing out on anything at all.

MAKES 4 SERVINGS

2 tablespoons coconut oil

1 small yellow onion, finely chopped

1 inch fresh ginger, peeled and grated

2 garlic cloves, minced

1 teaspoon cumin seeds

1/2 teaspoon ground coriander

2 teaspoons garam masala

1 teaspoon ground turmeric

1/2 teaspoon mustard seeds

Pinch of crushed red chile flakes (optional)

Sea salt, to taste

2 Medjool dates, pitted and chopped

One 15-ounce can chickpeas, drained and rinsed

1/4 cup chopped roasted peanuts

2 cups small cauliflower florets

Half of a 15-ounce can light coconut milk

2 cups cooked brown rice or cauliflower rice, to serve

2 tablespoons chopped fresh cilantro leaves, to garnish

1 tablespoon chopped fresh mint leaves, to garnish

4 scallions, thinly sliced, to garnish

HEAT the coconut oil in a large high-sided sauté pan over medium-high heat. Add the onion, ginger, and garlic and cook until softened, about 5 minutes, stirring often. Add the cumin seeds, coriander, garam masala, turmeric, mustard seeds, and chile flakes (if using), and toast for 1 minute. Season with salt. Add the dates, chickpeas, 2 tablespoons of the peanuts, and 1 cup water. Bring to a boil and reduce to a simmer. Let simmer for 10 minutes. Add the cauliflower florets and simmer until tender, 10 to 12 minutes. Remove from the heat and stir in the coconut milk. Let warm through.

SERVE the curry over the rice and garnish with the cilantro, mint, scallions, and the remaining 2 tablespoons peanuts.

Sunflower Seed Pesto Pasta with Charred Zucchini

The advent of truly delicious chickpea (and lentil!) pasta was a momentous occasion for me. It now meant I could eat pasta anytime. And even better, that this bowl of pasta would actually keep me quite full thanks to the additional fiber and protein.

My only complaint is that it can sometimes feel a tad dry, so I make sure to add a bit of extra sauce and bring in some freshness with vegetables when I can—adding fresh, peppery arugula to my pasta has been a major game changer! Kind of like salad pasta, rather than pasta salad. I know it sounds weird but trust me—it's so good.

When I have a little bit more time, I love taking the extra step of adding charred zucchini to this recipe—but you can skip it if you need a faster fix! Charring releases some of the zucchini's water, concentrates its flavor while keeping it juicy, and adds a little rich depth that goes nicely with the creamy, garlic-scented Sunflower Seed Cheeseless Pesto sauce.

MAKES 4 SERVINGS

Sea salt, to taste

1 pound chickpea or lentil penne, rotini, or other shaped noodle, or your favorite grain-free pasta

2 or 3 small zucchini, cut into ½-inch-thick coins

2 tablespoons extra-virgin olive oil

¾ to 1 cup Everyday Sunflower Seed Cheeseless Pesto (page 254)

A big handful or two of fresh arugula (optional)

Freshly cracked black pepper, to taste

3 tablespoons toasted pine nuts (see Toasting Nuts, Seeds, and Spices, page 199), to garnish

BRING a large pot of salted water to a boil. Add the pasta and cook according to the package instructions. Drain, reserving ½ cup of the pasta water.

HEAT a large cast-iron skillet over medium-high heat.

IN a medium bowl, toss the zucchini with the olive oil and season with salt. Place the zucchini coins in the hot skillet and char about 2 minutes on each side, then transfer to a plate (work in batches as needed to avoid overcrowding the pan and steaming).

IN a large bowl, combine the pasta and the Everyday Sunflower Seed Cheeseless Pesto. Toss until combined, adding splashes of the reserved pasta water as needed to help the pesto coat the pasta evenly. Add the zucchini coins and the arugula (if using), and gently toss to combine. Season with salt and pepper as desired. Serve garnished with the toasted pine nuts.

Mama's BBQ Chicken

Tell me this picture isn't calling your name with its total party-of-one vibes?? I made this one night using a leftover chicken drumstick from the kids' dinner. I splashed some BBQ sauce on top and let it roast until the chicken was hot and the sauce was sticky, glistening, and crusted in places. I've given you a technique to use here if you want to get the same result using fresh chicken, but keep this idea for a leftover remodel tucked away in your back pocket for some night in the not-so-distant future when you really deserve something good just for you.

MAKES 4 SERVINGS

---

8 bone-in, skin-on chicken thighs and/or 12 drumsticks

2 tablespoons plus 1 teaspoon extra-virgin olive oil

1 teaspoon fine sea salt, plus more to taste

2 cups Barbecue Sauce (page 261)

Freshly cracked black pepper, to taste

PREHEAT the oven to 425ºF. Place two sheet pans in the oven to preheat.

PAT all sides of the chicken very dry. Place in a large bowl and toss with 1 tablespoon of the olive oil to coat. Season with the salt. Toss in 1 cup of the barbecue sauce to coat. Divide the remaining 1 cup barbecue sauce: save half in a separate small bowl for serving and leave half in the large bowl to use for basting throughout the cooking process, to avoid cross-contamination.

REMOVE the sheet pans from the oven and carefully grease each with 2 teaspoons of the olive oil using a heat-resistant brush. Carefully place the marinated chicken pieces skin side down about an inch apart on the hot pans (they should sizzle!). Bake for 20 to 25 minutes, rotating the pans halfway through, until the sauce begins to caramelize. Flip the chicken pieces over to be skin side up and baste with some of the remaining barbecue sauce. Roast for another 10 to 20 minutes or until a meat thermometer registers 165ºF.

PREHEAT the broiler. If there is a significant amount of oil and fat rendered on the sheet pan, transfer the chicken to a clean sheet pan to avoid sparking a flame under the broiler. Brush the chicken once more with the remaining barbecue sauce. Place the chicken on the top oven rack under the broiler, about 5 inches from the heat source, and broil until the saucy skin crisps and caramelizes, 2 to 3 minutes, watching so it doesn't burn. The skin's surface should be sticky and deeply dark golden brown—yum!

LET rest for 5 to 10 minutes to allow the juices to distribute evenly. Serve with the small bowl of the reserved barbecue sauce on the side for dipping. Savor your special moment!

Sheet-Pan Miso-Glazed Sea Bass with Roasted Bok Choy

Another sheet-pan wonder! This one is extra fast because the fish cooks up quickly. The miso caramelizes beautifully into a wonderful, sticky-sweet and fermented crust that definitely gives this dish an "I worked all day on it!" quality—but the recipe is super easy. The sauce is flavorful and tasty and the bass is a particularly mild white fish, so this is a great way to dip your toe into seafood if you're not totally sure you love the flavor. This recipe also works great with shrimp. You'll just want to watch the cook time to make sure you pull them out of the oven as soon as they curl into that loose C shape.

--- **MAKES 4 SERVINGS** ---

SEA BASS AND BOK CHOY

2 tablespoons grapeseed oil

Four 5- to 6-ounce skin-on sea bass fillets

4 baby bok choy heads, trimmed and cut in half lengthwise

½ bunch scallions, white and light green parts only, thinly sliced on the bias, to garnish

1 Fresno chile, thinly sliced, to garnish

MISO MARINADE

¼ cup white or yellow miso paste

1 tablespoon toasted sesame oil

1 tablespoon rice vinegar

2 teaspoons tamari or coconut aminos

Juice from 1 lime (about 2 tablespoons)

2 teaspoons Date Syrup (page 244)

PREHEAT the oven to 425ºF. Line a sheet pan with parchment paper and brush with 1 tablespoon of the grapeseed oil.

TO make the miso marinade, whisk the miso paste, toasted sesame oil, rice vinegar, tamari, lime juice, and Date Syrup in a medium bowl.

BRUSH the top and sides of the sea bass with half of the marinade and place the fillets on the prepared sheet pan. Toss the bok choy in the remaining marinade and arrange it around the sea bass in a single layer. Drizzle the remaining tablespoon of grapeseed oil over the bok choy.

ROAST for 10 to 14 minutes, or to desired doneness. The fish is cooked when it is opaque and flakes easily with a fork. The bok choy should be tender and lightly golden. Garnish with the scallions and Fresno chile and serve.

Feel-Good Turkey Meatloaf

Why am I so in love with meatloaf? I just really think in some ways (many ways) it's the perfect comfort food. I love it hot out of the oven and cold the next day on open-faced sandwiches. I love it for family meals and for dinner parties. When you can keep it light but still get all the pleasure of enjoying a meal that every member of your household is going to crave, that's a home run in my book.

Zucchini keeps the turkey blend moist and flavorful, beans add extra heft and protein, and fresh herbs keep it very me. A fast ketchup-style sauce with tomato paste, vinegar, and Date Syrup for the glaze is my little gift to you and healthy meatloaf lovers everywhere who need to see that glistening, sticky-sweet coating to really be satisfied.

MAKES 4 TO 6 SERVINGS

MEATLOAF

3 tablespoons extra-virgin olive oil

1 small sweet or yellow onion, finely chopped

2 garlic cloves, minced

1 tablespoon fresh thyme leaves

1 teaspoon dried oregano

½ teaspoon dried basil

1 cup shredded zucchini

2 pounds ground turkey (preferably a mix of light and dark meat)

¼ cup finely chopped fresh parsley leaves

½ cup mashed pinto beans

1 cup almond flour

1 large egg, lightly beaten

⅓ cup Nut Milk, using almonds (page 62)

2 teaspoons tamari or coconut aminos

1¼ teaspoons sea salt

¼ teaspoon freshly cracked black pepper

TOMATO PASTE GLAZE

¼ cup tomato paste

2 tablespoons apple cider vinegar

1 tablespoon Date Syrup (page 244)

PREHEAT the oven to 375ºF. Line a sheet pan with parchment paper and grease with 1 tablespoon of the olive oil.

TO make the meatloaf, heat the remaining 2 tablespoons olive oil in a medium sauté pan over medium heat. Add the onion and garlic and sauté until softened and golden, about 6 minutes. Add the thyme, oregano, and basil and cook another minute. Remove from the heat and let cool completely.

PLACE the shredded zucchini in a clean kitchen towel and wring it out to release the excess moisture. In a large bowl, combine the zucchini, ground turkey, cooled onion mixture, parsley, beans, almond flour, egg, Nut Milk, tamari, salt, and pepper and mix with a wooden spoon until

(recipe continues)

just combined. Form into a 5 x 11-inch loaf on the prepared sheet pan. Tent with foil and bake for 40 minutes.

MEANWHILE, make the tomato paste glaze. Whisk together the tomato paste, vinegar, and Date Syrup in a small bowl.

BRUSH the meatloaf with the glaze and return it, without the foil tent, to the oven for 15 to 20 minutes, until it registers 160ºF on a meat thermometer and the glaze is caramelized.

LET rest for 10 to 15 minutes. Slice and serve.

Soy-Ginger Turkey Meatballs with Miso Sweet Potato Noodles

One thing I especially love about meatballs is that they are conveniently bite-size and wonderfully generous in the surface area department, so the ratio of deeply golden brown, crisp exterior to flavorful, moist interior is spot-on. This fragrant Soy-Ginger Turkey Meatball tastes something like the tender inside of a dumpling. I love it over sauteed Sweet Potato Noodles or rice noodles, or eaten alone with some crisp cucumber slices and a little Sweet Chili Soy Dressing (page 275).

———— **MAKES 16 MEATBALLS** ————

SOY-GINGER MEATBALLS

1 tablespoon toasted sesame oil

2 scallions, minced

1 inch fresh ginger, peeled and grated

2 garlic cloves, minced

1 pound ground turkey (or ground chicken)

½ cup almond flour

1 large egg, lightly beaten

1 tablespoon tamari or coconut aminos

½ teaspoon sea salt

¼ teaspoon freshly cracked pepper

2 tablespoons grapeseed oil

SWEET POTATO NOODLES

2 teaspoons toasted sesame oil

2 inches fresh ginger, peeled and grated

2 garlic cloves, grated

¼ cup white or yellow miso paste

2 teaspoons tamari or coconut aminos

2 teaspoons freshly squeezed lime juice

2 tablespoons grapeseed oil

4 medium Japanese yams (2 pounds total), peeled and spiralized into noodles or 2 pounds store-bought sweet potato noodles

Sea salt, to taste

3 scallions, white and light green parts only, thinly sliced, to garnish

Chili Sesame Oil (page 253), to garnish

TO make the meatballs, heat the sesame oil in a medium sauté pan over medium-low heat. Add the scallions, ginger, and garlic and cook, stirring often, until softened, about 2 minutes. Remove from the heat and let cool completely in the pan.

IN a large bowl, mix the ground turkey, cooled scallion mixture, almond flour, egg, tamari, salt, and pepper until just combined. Form into sixteen 1½-inch meatballs.

(recipe continues)

TO BAKE THE MEATBALLS

PREHEAT the oven to 400°F. Line a sheet pan with foil and grease with 1 tablespoon of the grapeseed oil.

PLACE the meatballs 1 inch apart on the prepared sheet pan. Brush with the remaining 1 tablespoon grapeseed oil. Bake for 16 to 18 minutes, until cooked through and a meat thermometer registers an internal temperature of 165°F.

TO SEAR THE MEATBALLS

HEAT the grapeseed oil in a large sauté pan over medium-high heat. Add the meatballs and sear on all sides until golden brown and cooked through, 8 to 10 minutes, until a meat thermometer registers an internal temperature of 165°F. Transfer the meatballs to a plate, spreading them in a single layer so they don't steam. Loosely cover with foil to keep them warm until ready to serve.

WIPE out the sauté pan to use for the sweet potato noodles. Set aside.

TO make the noodles, whisk the sesame oil, ginger, garlic, miso paste, tamari, lime juice, and ½ cup warm water in a medium bowl until smooth. Set aside.

HEAT the grapeseed oil in the sauté pan over medium-high heat. Add the sweet potato noodles and cook, using tongs to toss often, until softened but still slightly al dente, about 5 minutes. Season with salt. Add the sauce, toss to coat, and heat through, about 2 minutes.

DIVIDE the noodles among four plates and top each with 4 meatballs. Garnish with the sliced scallions and a drizzle of Chili Sesame Oil.

Sicilian-ish Bison Meatballs in Tomato Sauce

What is Sicilian-ish, you might ask? The happy little island of Sicily, off the coast of Italy, is famous for pairing briny, bitter, sour, and sweet flavors together, resulting in dishes like caponata that evolve and delight, bite after bite. Their jubilant use of capers and currants and tender pine nuts and anchovies is extremely inspiring to me. However, I'm not sure the grandmothers of Sicily would approve of almond flour (or bison) in their family recipe for meatballs, so I'm adding the "-ish" to allow for some liberties.

These meatballs feel full of surprises with little pops of sweet currants, bursts of fat from the pockets of pecorino and pine nuts, and the tiniest hint of citrus from the lemon zest. I've also included cooking options both for nights when you want to lavish a little extra time searing and crisping the meatballs and nights when baking a whole tray off in the oven is more your speed.

MAKES 16 MEATBALLS

TOMATO SAUCE

1 tablespoon extra-virgin olive oil

1 small yellow onion, finely chopped

½ teaspoon sea salt, plus more to taste

2 garlic cloves, minced

1 teaspoon fresh thyme leaves

½ teaspoon dried oregano

One 28-ounce can whole peeled San Marzano tomatoes, crushed with your hands

Freshly cracked black pepper, to taste

1 cup loosely packed fresh whole basil leaves, torn, plus more for garnish

SICILIAN-ISH MEATBALLS

3 tablespoons extra-virgin olive oil

½ cup yellow onion, finely chopped

2 garlic cloves, minced

1 teaspoon fresh thyme leaves

½ teaspoon dried oregano

1 pound ground bison (or ground lamb)

2 tablespoons toasted pine nuts (see Toasting Nuts, Seeds, and Spices, page 199)

2 teaspoons dried currants

½ cup almond flour

⅓ cup grated Pecorino Romano cheese, plus more for garnish

Zest of ½ lemon (about 1 teaspoon)

1 large egg, lightly beaten

½ teaspoon sea salt

¼ teaspoon freshly cracked black pepper, to taste

TO make the tomato sauce, heat the olive oil in a medium heavy-bottomed pot over medium-high heat. Add the onion and salt and cook until softened, 5 to 6 minutes, stirring occasionally. Add the garlic, thyme, and oregano during the last minute of cooking, stirring regularly to combine and prevent burning. Add the tomatoes and stir to combine. Fill the tomato can with 1 cup water and add it to the pot. Let simmer while making the meatballs, about 20 minutes. If the sauce gets too thick, add a bit of water, a few tablespoons at a time. Once cooked, remove the sauce from the heat and reserve, seasoning with salt and pepper as desired. Stir in the basil right before serving.

TO make the meatballs, heat a medium sauté pan over medium-high heat and add 1 tablespoon of the olive oil. Add the onion and garlic and cook until softened, 4 to 5 minutes. Add the thyme and oregano and cook another minute. Remove from the heat and let cool completely in the pan.

IN a large bowl, mix the ground bison, cooled onion mixture, pine nuts, currants, almond flour, Pecorino Romano, lemon zest, egg, salt, and pepper until just combined. Roll into sixteen 1½-inch meatballs.

TO BAKE THE MEATBALLS

PREHEAT the oven to 400ºF. Line a sheet pan with foil and grease with 1 tablespoon of the olive oil.

PLACE the meatballs 1 inch apart on the prepared sheet pan. Brush with the remaining 1 tablespoon olive oil. Bake for 16 to 18 minutes, until cooked through and a meat thermometer registers an internal temperature of 165ºF. Add the meatballs to the tomato sauce and toss to coat.

TO SEAR THE MEATBALLS

HEAT the remaining 2 tablespoons olive oil in a large sauté pan over medium-high heat. Add the meatballs and sear on all sides until golden brown, 6 to 8 minutes.

WHEN ready to serve, place the meatballs in the reserved tomato sauce and simmer until cooked through and a meat thermometer registers an internal temperature of 160ºF, 13 to 15 minutes.

SERVE 4 meatballs per person with a ladle of the tomato sauce. Garnish with additional Pecorino Romano and freshly torn basil.

Chipotle Chicken Meatball Burrito Bowl

I love the way this hearty combo comes together. Using chicken (or turkey) for the meatballs keeps them light and plenty spicy with the chipotle in adobo. The meatballs themselves are so flavorful, I saved us some time and kept the rest of the rice and beans in the bowl simple. I love to top this dish with a few crisp, crunchy, sweet plantain chips—but you can easily leave those off if they feel like they're too much. I am a big believer that occasional, meaningful indulgences fuel my resolve to eat well the rest of the time, and this is one such place where a little bit of sin does a lot of delicious good.

— MAKES 16 MEATBALLS —

CHIPOTLE CHICKEN MEATBALLS

3 tablespoons extra-virgin olive oil

½ cup finely chopped red onion

2 garlic cloves, minced

½ teaspoon ground cumin

1 chipotle in adobo, minced

1 pound ground chicken (or ground turkey)

2 tablespoons chopped fresh cilantro leaves and tender stems

½ cup almond flour

1 large egg, lightly beaten

½ teaspoon sea salt

¼ teaspoon freshly cracked black pepper

BURRITO BOWL

¼ cup coconut oil

1 ripe plantain, peeled and sliced thin to make chips

Sea salt, to taste

2 cups cooked brown rice

One 15-ounce can black beans, drained, rinsed, and warmed

1 recipe Pico de Gallo (page 249) or jarred salsa with no added sugar

1 avocado, cut into medium dice

1 to 2 tablespoons chopped pickled jalapeños, to garnish (optional)

2 tablespoons chopped fresh cilantro, to garnish

TO make the meatballs, heat a small sauté pan over medium-high heat with 1 tablespoon of the olive oil. Add the red onion and garlic and cook until softened, about 4 minutes. Add the cumin and chipotle in adobo and cook for another minute. Remove from the heat and let cool completely in the pan.

IN a large bowl, mix the ground chicken, cooled onion mixture, cilantro, almond flour, egg, salt, and pepper until just combined. Form into sixteen 1½-inch meatballs.

TO BAKE THE MEATBALLS

PREHEAT the oven to 400ºF. Line a sheet pan with foil and grease with 1 tablespoon of the olive oil.

PLACE the meatballs 1 inch apart on the prepared sheet pan. Brush with the remaining 1 tablespoon olive oil. Bake for 16 to 18 minutes, until cooked through and a meat thermometer registers an internal temperature of 165ºF.

TO SEAR THE MEATBALLS

HEAT the remaining 2 tablespoons olive oil in a large sauté pan over medium-high heat. Add the meatballs and sear on all sides until golden brown and cooked through, 8 to 10 minutes, until a meat thermometer registers an internal temperature of 165ªF. Cover the pan, remove it from the heat, and set it aside to keep warm.

LINE a plate with paper towels.

HEAT the coconut oil in a large cast-iron skillet or high-sided sauté pan over medium-high heat. Add the plantains and fry until golden brown and crunchy, 3 to 4 minutes. Transfer to the paper towel–lined plate and season with salt.

TO assemble, divide the brown rice among four bowls. Top with equal amounts of black beans, Pico de Gallo, avocado, plantain chips, and meatballs. Garnish with the pickled jalapeños (if using) and cilantro and serve.

Chicken and Scallion Cabbage Dumplings

Save this recipe for a day you feel like crafting while cooking. Rolling the cabbage leaves around fragrant little mounds of ground chicken scented with ginger, garlic, and soy can be its own form of meditation. And while I do love this simple, meaty mix, it is only the beginning! Try adding grated carrots or zucchini (just wring any excess water out in a clean dishtowel before adding) or finely chopped shiitake mushrooms for an extra umami boost.

When it comes time to tuck into a piping hot plate of these beautifully packaged little gems, glide each dumpling through your personal side of Sweet Chili Soy Dressing, and enjoy the deeply gratifying experience of popping it into your mouth for a total taste explosion.

─── **MAKES 12 DUMPLINGS** ───

1 cabbage head, Savoy or napa preferred (see Want to Use Green Cabbage to Wrap Your Dumplings?, opposite, if using green cabbage)

1 pound ground chicken

3 scallions, white and light green parts only, thinly sliced

1 inch fresh ginger, peeled and grated

2 garlic cloves, grated

¼ teaspoon crushed red chile flakes

1 tablespoon tamari or coconut aminos

1 teaspoon toasted sesame oil

½ teaspoon sea salt

Freshly cracked black pepper, to taste

Sweet Chili Soy Dressing (page 275), to serve

Chili Sesame Oil (page 253), to serve

LAY out a large dishtowel or line a sheet pan with paper towels and set aside.

BRING a medium pot of salted water to a boil. If using Savoy or napa cabbage, remove the stem and carefully separate 15 of the largest leaves (though only 12 are needed, it's always good to have backups!). If using green cabbage, see Want to Use Green Cabbage to Wrap Your Dumplings?, opposite.

MEANWHILE, in a medium bowl, combine the ground chicken, scallions, ginger, garlic, chile flakes, tamari, sesame oil, salt, and a few cracks of black pepper, and gently mix just to combine. Set aside.

WHEN the water is boiling, use tongs to submerge a few cabbage leaves at a time into the water, just until tender and pliable, 30 to 60 seconds. Transfer to the dishtowel or prepared sheet pan and continue working in batches until all the leaves have been blanched. Let cool until easy to handle and pat away any surface liquid with additional paper towels.

TO roll each dumpling, place a cabbage leaf in front of you with the core pointing toward you. If the cabbage leaf has a tough or thick core, slice that portion away with a paring knife. Scoop 1 to 2 tablespoons (depending on how large your cabbage leaves are and how much they can hold; just make sure the dumplings are uniform in size so they cook evenly) of the chicken mixture into the center of the leaf about ½ inch from the bottom. Fold the right and left sides toward the center to enclose the meat on either end, then fold the bottom up over the sides and continue rolling away from you like you would a jelly roll. Place on a plate seam side down and continue with the remaining cabbage leaves until all the chicken mixture is used.

ADD 1 to 2 inches of water in a large pot with a steamer basket (make sure the liquid is not touching the bottom of the steamer basket or you will get soggy dumplings) and heat the water over medium-high heat until gently simmering. Carefully add the dumplings to the steamer basket seam side down (layering if needed). Turn the heat to high. When the water is boiling, cover the pot and steam the dumplings for 10 minutes, or until the filling is cooked and registers an internal temperature of 165°F on a meat thermometer.

SERVE with the Sweet Chili Soy Dressing and Chili Sesame Oil.

WANT TO USE GREEN CABBAGE TO WRAP YOUR DUMPLINGS?

Green cabbage is a bit tougher and requires thorough boiling—which takes time and saps nutrients—to get the leaves pliable enough to peel away intact and then bend around springy bundles of fragrant meat. But sometimes green cabbage is all I can find, and that's when I use this technique. Boil a large pot of water over high heat. Add the whole head of cabbage and cook until softened, 10 to 12 minutes. Remove and let it cool until you can handle it, then cut out the core and carefully pull away 15 large outer leaves. Scatter them over a clean dishtowel or paper towels to dry. Pat away any surface liquid with additional paper towels. Proceed to fill, roll, and steam!

Crispy Tofu with Candied Brussels Sprouts

Brussels sprouts are one of those extremely polarizing vegetables that I was determined to make delicious.

I set out to make a version in which they could be "candied" but healthy, crisp but not crispy, and—in combination with the tofu—a delicious carrier for some silky, spicy ginger-scallion tamari sauce. Tiny cabbage head makeover complete!

One 14-ounce container firm tofu, drained

¼ cup grapeseed oil

1 pound Brussels sprouts, trimmed and halved or quartered depending on size

2 tablespoons Date Syrup (page 244)

Sea salt, to taste

¼ to ½ teaspoon tapioca flour

Chili Sesame Oil (page 253), to serve

1 tablespoon toasted sesame seeds (see Toasting Nuts, Seeds, and Spices, page 199), to serve

GINGER-SCALLION TAMARI SAUCE

2 scallions, white and light green parts only, finely chopped

2 garlic cloves, grated

¼ cup tamari or coconut aminos

2 tablespoons rice vinegar

¼ teaspoon crushed red chile flakes

1 tablespoon Date Syrup (page 244)

PLACE the tofu on a plate lined with paper towels. Place another paper towel, plate, and a pot or cans of beans on top to weigh down the tofu and release any excess liquid for 10 minutes. Pat the tofu very dry and cut it into 1-inch cubes.

MEANWHILE, make the ginger-scallion tamari sauce. In a small bowl, whisk together the scallions, garlic, tamari, rice vinegar, chile flakes, and Date Syrup until smooth. Toss with the tofu cubes and marinate for at least 15 minutes or up to overnight, covered and refrigerated.

WHEN ready to cook, heat 2 tablespoons of the grapeseed oil in a large cast-iron skillet over medium-high heat. Add the Brussels sprouts cut side down and cook until golden brown and tender but with some crunch on the bottom, about 6 minutes. Add the Date Syrup during the last couple of minutes of cooking, toss to combine, and let caramelize on the Brussels sprouts. Season with salt. Remove the sprouts to a plate.

REMOVE the tofu from the marinade, reserving any excess marinade. Heat the remaining 2 tablespoons of grapeseed oil in the pan over medium heat. Add the tofu and sear on all sides until golden brown and crisp, carefully turning with tongs to make sure all sides are evenly browned, 7 to 9 minutes total.

IN a small bowl, whisk 1 tablespoon water with the tapioca flour to make a slurry. Add the reserved marinade and slurry to the pan and toss to coat the tofu, letting the sauce thicken, about a minute. Return the sprouts to the pan and toss everything to combine and heat through. Serve garnished with the Chili Sesame Oil and toasted sesame seeds.

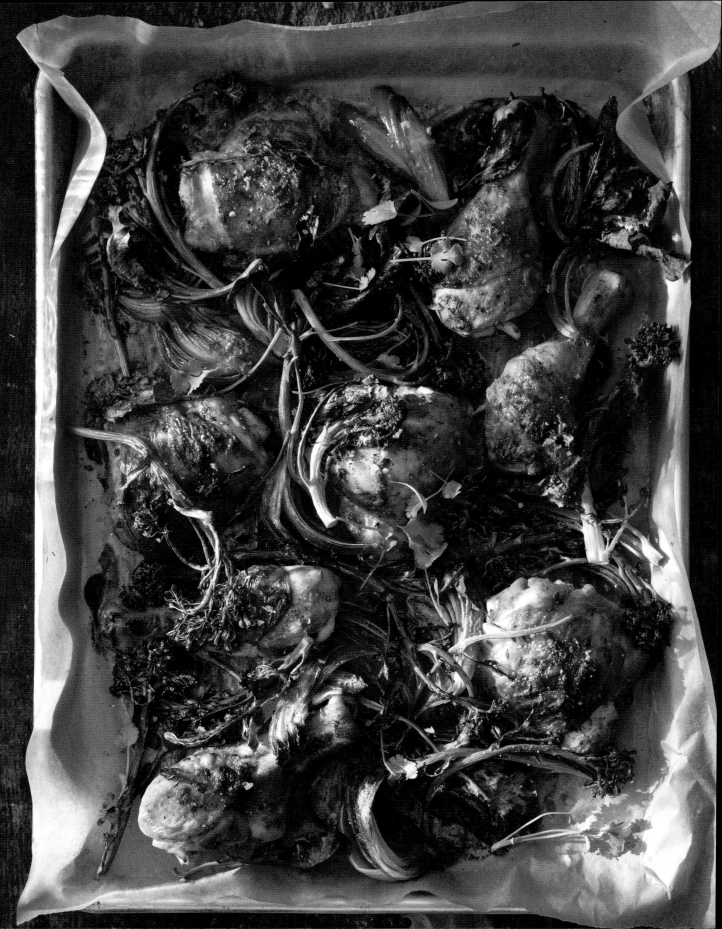

Sheet-Pan Tandoori Chicken with Broccoli

Prepare for a wondrously colorful sheet-pan dinner you can just tell will be a mouth party. Chicken gets a bath in spiced yogurt so it stays fragrant and juicy. Broccoli gets tender and deep golden brown. Charred red onions turn sweet and soft.

Swap in bone-in chicken breast to keep it extra light but still juicy. Reduce the cooking time slightly so it doesn't dry out.

— MAKES 4 SERVINGS —

2 garlic cloves, minced

1 inch fresh ginger, peeled and grated

1 tablespoon garam masala

2 teaspoons chili powder

2 teaspoons cumin seeds

1 teaspoon ground turmeric

1 teaspoon sweet paprika

1 cup full-fat goat or sheep milk yogurt

Zest and juice from 1 lime (about 1 teaspoon zest and 2 tablespoons juice)

1¼ teaspoons sea salt, plus more to taste

4 bone-in, skin-on chicken thighs

4 chicken drumsticks

3 tablespoons extra-virgin olive oil

6 cups bite-size broccoli florets

1 red onion, halved, each half sliced into 6 wedges

Freshly cracked black pepper, to taste

2 tablespoons chopped fresh cilantro, to garnish

1 lime, halved

IN a small bowl, whisk the garlic, ginger, garam masala, chili powder, cumin seeds, turmeric, paprika, yogurt, lime zest and juice, and ¾ teaspoon of the salt until smooth.

PLACE the chicken in a zip-top bag or baking dish and toss with the sauce mixture. Seal the bag or cover the dish and marinate for at least 1 hour and up to overnight in the refrigerator.

WHEN ready to roast, preheat the oven to 425°F. Line two sheet pans with parchment paper and grease with 1 tablespoon of the olive oil. Remove the chicken from the refrigerator and let it sit at room temperature for 10 to 15 minutes.

IN a large bowl, toss the remaining 2 tablespoons olive oil and ½ teaspoon salt with the broccoli florets and the red onion until lightly coated.

REMOVE the chicken from the bag, allowing any excess marinade to drip off, and place on the prepared sheet pans. Scatter the broccoli around the chicken, taking care not to overcrowd the pans.

BAKE for 35 to 40 minutes, rotating the pans top to bottom and front to back halfway through, until the chicken is cooked through and registers an internal temperature of 165°F on a meat thermometer. Turn the broiler on and broil for 3 to 5 minutes, until the chicken skin is browned and crispy.

SEASON with salt and pepper as desired. Garnish with the chopped cilantro and a squeeze of fresh lime and serve.

Braised Chicken Thighs with Fennel, Lemon, and Dates

A little twist on honey mustard chicken, this is the perfect pot to put on as the weather starts to chill. As they simmer away, the chicken thighs drink up the stock fortified with dates, onions, and fennel. When everything is succulent and ready to be devoured, remove the chicken from the pot and whisk a touch of mustard into the remaining sauce before ladling it over everyone's portion. I love the extra bite it brings.

———— **MAKES 4 SERVINGS** ————

2 tablespoons extra-virgin olive oil

1½ pounds bone-in, skin-on chicken thighs

½ teaspoon sea salt, plus more to taste

1 small yellow onion, thinly sliced

1 fennel head, fronds removed and discarded, cored and thinly sliced

1 lemon, thinly sliced into wheels

2 cups chicken stock

3 Medjool dates, pitted and roughly chopped

2 teaspoons Dijon mustard

2 tablespoons chopped fresh parsley, to garnish

Freshly cracked black pepper, to taste

HEAT the olive oil in a large heavy-bottomed pot or Dutch oven over medium-high heat. Season the chicken thighs on both sides with the salt. Add the chicken thighs, skin side down, to the skillet and cook until golden brown, about 5 minutes. Flip and cook until golden brown on the other side, another 3 to 4 minutes. Transfer to a plate. The chicken will not be fully cooked at this point. It will finish as it braises.

ADD the onion and fennel to the pot, season with a pinch of salt, and sauté until just softened, about 5 minutes. Add the lemon slices and deglaze the pot with the chicken stock, scraping the browned bits up from the bottom. Return the chicken thighs to the pot and sprinkle the dates around. Reduce the heat to a simmer and partially cover the pot. Simmer for 12 to 15 minutes, until the chicken thighs are cooked through and a meat thermometer registers an internal temperature of 165°F.

REMOVE the pot from the heat and place the chicken thighs on a serving plate. Stir the Dijon mustard into the sauce. Ladle the sauce over the chicken and garnish with the parsley and pepper.

Roasted Butternut Squash Pasta Bake

I am always amazed at how lusciously creamy this sauce gets. Butternut squash loses some of its moisture and becomes even sweeter as it roasts, and paired with Manchego and the salty bite of pecorino, it whips up to smooth, silky perfection. Needless to say, I am very happy to sit down with a deep bowl of this knowing I'm eating mostly vegetables and chickpeas but feeling like I'm eating utter decadence. I leave a few cubes of squash whole—little steamy pillows to bite into every once in a while—and I like topping my bowl with a few chopped walnuts just to add some extra toasty texture.

— MAKES 4 TO 6 SERVINGS —

2 tablespoons extra-virgin olive oil

1 medium butternut squash, peeled, seeded, and cut into ½-inch chunks (about 8 cups)

1 shallot, finely chopped

2 garlic cloves, minced

1 tablespoon chopped fresh sage leaves

½ teaspoon sea salt, plus more to taste

1 pound chickpea rigatoni

2 cups chicken stock, warmed

½ cup Nut Milk, using almonds (page 62)

¾ cup shredded Manchego cheese

Freshly cracked black pepper, to taste

2 tablespoons grated Pecorino Romano

¼ cup walnuts, toasted and chopped (see Toasting Nuts, Seeds, and Spices, page 199), to garnish

PREHEAT the oven to 425ºF. Line a sheet pan with foil.

TOSS the olive oil, butternut squash, shallot, garlic, and sage in a large bowl until combined. Spread evenly on the prepared sheet pan and roast for 25 to 30 minutes, flipping halfway through, until the squash is tender.

MEANWHILE, bring a large pot of salted water to a boil. Cook the pasta for half of the package instruction time. Drain and rinse with cold water. Set aside.

REDUCE the oven temperature to 350ºF. Reserve a third of the roasted squash cubes.

PLACE the remaining two-thirds of the squash cubes in a high-speed blender with the chicken stock, Nut Milk, and Manchego and puree until smooth (this may need to be done in batches). Transfer to a large bowl and toss with the pasta and reserved squash cubes. Season with salt and pepper as desired.

PLACE the mixture in a 9 x 13-inch baking dish and sprinkle with the pecorino. Cover with foil and bake for 15 minutes, then uncover and bake another 10 minutes, until the cheese is golden and the top of the noodles is crispy. Serve garnished with chopped walnuts.

Crispy Chicken Strips with Sweet and Spicy Mustard

If you live with many small children like I do, I'm sure you're used to a steady parade of chicken fingers. I knew there had to be a way to use them to my advantage. This is a great recipe to sneak some extra fiber, protein, and good brain-nourishing fats into food they (and you!) really want to eat.

Extra chicken strips are perfect to use for Poblano Chopped Chicken Salad with Creamy Cilantro-Lime Dressing (page 270).

───────────── **MAKES 4 SERVINGS** ─────────────

Pure extra-virgin olive oil spray

½ cup whole flaxseeds

1 cup raw almonds

1 cup almond flour

1 tablespoon onion powder

Sea salt, to taste

2 large eggs, whisked

1 pound chicken breast tenders

Sweet and Spicy Mustard (page 251), to serve

PREHEAT the oven to 375ºF. Place a baking rack on a sheet pan and grease with the olive oil spray.

IN the bowl of a food processor fitted with the blade attachment, pulse the flaxseeds and raw almonds until finely ground but still textured.

PREPARE a dredging station with three shallow bowls. Place the almond flour in the first bowl, add the onion powder, and season with a pinch of salt. Place the eggs in the second bowl and season with a pinch of salt. Place the flaxseed-almond mixture in the third bowl and season with a pinch of salt.

DREDGE a chicken strip in the almond flour, shaking off any excess. Dip into the egg, then coat in the flaxseed-almond mixture, shaking off any excess. Place on the prepared baking rack. Repeat with the remaining chicken tenders. Spray the chicken tenders with olive oil spray and season with one last pinch of salt.

BAKE for 12 to 15 minutes, until cooked through, golden brown, and crunchy. Immediately and carefully remove the chicken strips from the hot rack.

SERVE with the Sweet and Spicy Mustard.

Barbecue Pulled Chicken on Crispy Smashed Japanese Yams

Oh man, these are good. Japanese yams are the kind of thing I always roast thinking I'm going to eat them for dinner, and then by the time I've spent an hour smelling them caramelizing in the oven into pudding-sweet confections, getting denser and softer by the minute, I can't even wait for them to cool before devouring slice after steaming slice as a snack while I make the rest of the meal. Plain or with a sprinkle of sea salt, they taste like dense, creamy candy and are so, so good for you.

At some point I realized you could smash and bake slices of Japanese yam and use them as crispy little edible saucers to top with barbecue pulled chicken. And honestly, now that you know this madness exists, why are you not on your way to shop for groceries immediately? Go now!

PS. I included the technique to make this in the slow cooker if you want to pop the ingredients in before you leave for work and have dinner ready and waiting when you get home.

MAKES 4 TO 6 SERVINGS

SMASHED JAPANESE YAMS

3 medium Japanese yams (about 1½ pounds), scrubbed

2 tablespoons extra-virgin olive oil

Sea salt and freshly cracked black pepper, to taste

PULLED CHICKEN

1½ teaspoons garlic powder

1 teaspoon onion powder

1 teaspoon dried thyme

1 teaspoon sweet paprika

1 teaspoon chili powder

½ teaspoon sea salt

2 boneless, skinless chicken breasts (about 1¼ pounds), cut into 2-inch chunks

2 boneless, skinless chicken thighs (about 8 ounces), cut into 2-inch chunks

2 tablespoons extra-virgin olive oil

1 small yellow onion, finely chopped

2 cups chicken stock (if using the stovetop method)

Barbecue Sauce (page 261)

2 teaspoons tapioca flour

TO make the smashed Japanese yams, preheat the oven to 425ºF. Line a sheet pan with foil. Prick the yams all over with the prongs of a fork. Wrap each yam in foil, place on the prepared sheet pan, and roast until tender, 35 to 40 minutes. Let cool until easy to handle.

BRUSH the foil-lined sheet pan with 1 tablespoon of the olive oil. Slice each yam into 1-inch-thick rounds. Place on the sheet pan and gently smash using the bottom of a cup. Drizzle with

(recipe continues)

the remaining 1 tablespoon olive oil and season with salt and pepper. Bake for 25 minutes, until golden and crispy, flipping halfway through.

TO make the pulled chicken, combine the garlic powder, onion powder, thyme, paprika, chili powder, and salt in a small bowl. Sprinkle the spice mixture over all sides of the chicken evenly.

TO MAKE THE CHICKEN ON THE STOVETOP

HEAT the olive oil in a large heavy-bottomed pot or Dutch oven over medium-high heat. Sear the chicken on all sides until browned, 7 to 8 minutes. Add the onion during the last couple of minutes of cooking. Deglaze the pan with the chicken stock, scraping up the browned bits from the bottom of the pan. Bring to a boil and reduce to a simmer. Cover and simmer for 7 to 10 minutes, until the chicken is tender and easy to shred.

SHRED the chicken using two forks, add the Barbecue Sauce, and stir to evenly coat and warm through. In a small bowl, whisk the tapioca flour with 2 teaspoons water until smooth. Stir the slurry into the chicken mixture and cook over low heat until thickened, about 2 minutes.

TO MAKE THE CHICKEN WITH A SLOW COOKER

PLACE the chicken in a 6-quart slow cooker and pour in the Barbecue Sauce. Add ¼ to ½ cup water or chicken stock to cover the chicken. Cover and set on high for 3 to 4 hours or low for 6 to 8 hours, until the chicken is cooked through.

IN the final hour of cooking, whisk the tapioca flour with 2 tablespoons water in a small bowl. Pour into the slow cooker, stir to combine, and finish cooking.

TO FINISH

WHEN the chicken is pull-apart tender and the sauce is thickened, shred the chicken with two forks.

MOUND portions of the pulled chicken onto the yam disks and feel free to spoon any little bit of leftover juices over the tops so every bite is good and juicy.

Vegan Spaghetti Squash Carbonara with Mushroom Bacon

If you or the people you're feeding hold the belief that "vegan" and "carbonara" are two words that cannot be successfully paired, think again.

This (admittedly) insane combination of silken tofu (!), cashews (!!), nutritional yeast (!!!), and sauerkraut brine (!!!!) makes for a sauce so decadent, so rich with umami, you'll be too busy happily slurping up noodles to ever wonder how something so truly bizarre could taste this delicious.

Using spaghetti squash as the noodle makes this bowl incredibly waistline friendly, though you could absolutely use shirataki noodles or another gluten-free noodle of your choosing. I like to top our bowls with crispy mushrooms I pretend are bacon, with a touch of cayenne to keep each bite ever so slightly spicy. Maybe it isn't carbonara, but it's damn tasty.

MAKES 4 SERVINGS

CARBONARA

1 medium spaghetti squash, split in half and seeded

¼ cup plus 1 teaspoon extra-virgin olive oil

¼ teaspoon sea salt, plus more to taste

½ cup nutritional yeast

12 ounces silken tofu

2 to 3 mounded tablespoons mild white miso paste

½ cup raw cashews

½ cup sauerkraut brine or juice from half a lemon

1 to 2 tablespoons Date Syrup (page 244)

½ teaspoon smoked paprika

Pinch of cayenne (if you like it spicy, optional)

Freshly cracked black pepper, to taste

MUSHROOM "BACON" TOPPING

2 tablespoons extra-virgin olive oil

1 shallot, minced

2 cups shiitake mushrooms, stemmed and thinly sliced

Sea salt, to taste

PREHEAT the oven to 375ºF. Rub both halves of the squash with 1 teaspoon of the olive oil and season with the salt. Place on a sheet pan cut side down and roast until golden brown and tender, about 1 hour. Let cool for 10 minutes.

MEANWHILE, make the mushroom "bacon" topping and the sauce. Heat the olive oil in a large sauté pan over medium-high heat. Add the shallots and mushrooms and toss to coat in the oil. Let the mushrooms cook undisturbed for 2 to 3 minutes, until golden brown. Toss again and cook 2 minutes more, until crispy and browned. Season with salt to taste.

IN the bowl of a food processor fitted with the blade attachment, combine the nutritional yeast, tofu, miso paste, cashews, remaining ¼ cup olive oil, sauerkraut brine, Date Syrup, smoked paprika, and cayenne (if using). Blend until smooth, then season with salt and pepper and set aside.

WHEN the spaghetti squash is cool enough to handle, use two forks to scrape it into noodles. Add the squash and sauce to the same pan used to sauté the mushrooms and toss to combine over low heat until warmed through. Divide among four bowls and serve.

Delivery Chicken with Basil, Snow Peas, and Okra

This is one of my favorite fast and flavorful dinners when there's no time to waste. I use snow peas and okra here, but bell peppers and broccoli work really well, too. The sauce is silky, with a just-right balance of sweet and heat and pungent, savory flavors. I love serving the glossy chicken over fluffy cauliflower rice so that none of the sauce goes to waste.

--- MAKES 4 SERVINGS ---

2 tablespoons extra-virgin olive oil

4 boneless, skinless chicken breasts, cut into 1-inch cubes

1/2 teaspoon sea salt

2 scallions, white and light green parts only, finely chopped

1/2 serrano pepper, minced

1 cup snow peas, finely chopped

1 1/2 cups okra, sliced into 1/2-inch coins

1/2 cup fresh basil leaves, torn

GLAZE

3 tablespoons toasted sesame oil

6 tablespoons tamari or coconut aminos

1 tablespoon Date Syrup (page 244)

2 inches fresh ginger, peeled and grated

2 garlic cloves, grated

TO SERVE

4 cups cooked cauliflower rice or 2 cups cooked brown rice (optional)

Chili Sesame Oil (page 253)

Lime wedges

1 cup bean sprouts

1 jalapeño, thinly sliced

Additional torn fresh basil leaves

HEAT the olive oil in a large sauté pan over medium-high heat. Add the chicken in an even layer and season with the salt. Cook until lightly browned on all sides, 5 to 6 minutes.

ADD the scallions and serrano and toss to combine. Add the snow peas and okra and cook an additional minute or two, until slightly softened and crisp-tender.

MEANWHILE, make the glaze. Combine the sesame oil, tamari, Date Syrup, ginger, and garlic in a small bowl.

POUR the glaze over the chicken mixture and toss to coat. Reduce the heat to medium-low and let the mixture simmer until the sauce thickens and coats the vegetables, about 2 minutes. Add the basil and toss gently to wilt the leaves.

SERVE over cauliflower rice (if using). Garnish with the Chili Sesame Oil, lime wedges, bean sprouts, jalapeño, and basil leaves.

Spatchcock Chicken with Figs and Celery Root

Mastering a whole roast chicken was one of my proudest moments in the kitchen, but sometimes you need dinner ready faster than an hour and forty-five minutes from now. Enter spatchcocking. By removing the backbone of the bird and cracking the ribs and breastbone, you are able to lay it flat, increasing the surface area facing the heat and ensuring that it not only cooks faster with less risk of accidentally drying out, but the entire surface of the skin gets deeply golden brown and crispy. It's far and away an easier—and frequently more delicious—technique, even if it doesn't have the classic elegance of the whole roast bird. Ask your butcher to spatchcock a chicken for you, or see the technique in the tip on page 174. (PS. You can use this same technique to get your Thanksgiving turkey done in half the time.)

I love pretty much any roasted veggie alongside a gloriously spatchcocked chicken, but this particular combination of earthy, sweet figs and fresh celery root with citrus, olives, and lots of sweet red onions that cook in the rendering chicken fat is a particular favorite for its flair. It's the ultimate warm, cozy, elegant, easy, one-pan wonder!

———— **MAKES 4 SERVINGS** ————

8 small red onions or large shallots, halved and trimmed

1 large celery root, peeled and cut into 1-inch cubes

12 fresh mission figs or 4 ripe plums, pitted and quartered

1 navel orange, zest removed in strips, juiced

¼ cup extra-virgin olive oil

2½ teaspoons sea salt

One 4- to 5-pound chicken, spatchcocked

1 small bunch fresh herbs, such as thyme, oregano, or mint, or a mixture

1 cup Castelvetrano olives, smashed and pitted

½ cup white wine (or broth or water)

½ to 1 cup chicken stock

Sea salt and freshly cracked black pepper, to taste

PREHEAT the oven to 425°F.

COMBINE the onions, celery root, figs, and orange zest in a large bowl. Drizzle with the orange juice and 2 tablespoons of the olive oil and season with ½ teaspoon salt. Toss to evenly coat. Transfer the vegetables to a large roasting pan and spread in an even layer.

PAT the chicken very dry using paper towels. Season on both sides with the remaining 2 teaspoons salt and drizzle with the remaining 2 tablespoons olive oil. Arrange the chicken skin side up over the vegetables. Scatter the herbs all around the chicken and vegetables. Roast for 20 minutes.

(recipe continues)

REDUCE the oven temperature to 375ºF and add the olives to the roasting pan. Roast until the chicken is golden and crisp, the vegetables are tender, and the juices run clear when the chicken is pierced with the tip of a knife, about 35 minutes. A meat thermometer should register 160ºF in the thickest part of the leg. It will come up to 165ºF as it rests.

CAREFULLY transfer the chicken to a cutting board, tent it with foil, and let it rest for 10 to 15 minutes. Transfer the cooked vegetables to a large bowl.

WHILE the roasting pan is still hot, pour out and discard all but 2 tablespoons of the fat in the bottom of the pan. Place the roasting pan over medium heat and deglaze with the wine, broth, or water, whisking up all the flavorful browned bits from the bottom and sides of the pan. Let simmer until reduced by half, about 2 minutes. Add the chicken stock and whisk to combine. Let simmer another minute or two, until the stock is warmed through and slightly reduced. Cut the chicken into pieces. Serve the chicken and vegetables with a drizzle of the delicious warm wine pan sauce over the top. Season with salt and pepper as desired.

LET'S TALK SPATCHCOCK!

While you absolutely could ask your butcher to spatchcock (aka remove the backbone and lay the poultry flat) for you, here's how to do it all on your own to maximize crispy, golden skin and get juicy roast bird every time! To spatchcock, get your sturdiest pair of kitchen shears and use them to cut along both sides of the bird's backbone so it can be removed. Discard the backbone (or keep for homemade stock or gravy or just to roast separately; the meat is ultratender). Flip the poultry over so it is breast side up, then firmly press down on the breast plate using the heel of your hand to crack the breastbone and allow the entire bird to lay flat. Season and roast as usual, but prepare to be ready to dine in about half the cooking time!

Carrot-Ginger Shrimp Bowl

Blackening is maybe my favorite way to cook any light protein, and I love how fresh, tender shrimp take on the blackening spices of thyme, oregano, and paprika. I serve these shrimp over brown rice and romaine lettuce tossed with cucumbers, shaved jalapeño, tons of herbs, and a bright Carrot-Ginger Dressing. It's crunchy, light, and refreshing with just enough heft and kick to fill you up and keep you hungry for more!

MAKES 4 SERVINGS

BLACKENED SHRIMP

1 tablespoon sweet paprika

1 teaspoon chili powder

¾ teaspoon garlic powder

1 teaspoon dried thyme

1 teaspoon dried oregano

Pinch of cayenne pepper

¼ teaspoon freshly cracked black pepper

½ teaspoon sea salt

1 pound shrimp, peeled and deveined, tails left on

2 tablespoons extra-virgin olive oil

BOWL

2 cups warm cooked brown rice or millet

2 romaine lettuce hearts, shredded

2 Persian cucumbers, finely chopped

1 avocado, diced (optional)

½ cup Carrot-Ginger Dressing (page 269)

¼ cup fresh mint leaves, torn

¼ cup fresh basil leaves, torn

½ bunch scallions, thinly sliced

1 jalapeño, thinly sliced (optional)

Lime wedges, to serve

LINE a plate with paper towels.

TO make the blackened shrimp, combine the paprika, chili powder, garlic powder, thyme, oregano, cayenne, black pepper, and salt in a medium bowl. Add the shrimp and toss to coat, shaking off any excess.

HEAT a large sauté pan with the olive oil over medium heat. Add the shrimp and sear until opaque, pink, and just cooked through, about 2 minutes per side. Transfer to the prepared plate.

TO assemble, arrange equal portions of the cooked rice, romaine, cucumbers, and avocado (if using) in four bowls. Drizzle the Carrot-Ginger Dressing on top and toss to lightly coat. Top each with one-quarter of the warm shrimp, then scatter each bowl with mint, basil, scallions, and jalapeño (if using). Serve with lime wedges.

Lamb Chops with Cilantro-Peanut Chutney and White Beans

John, my brother Oliver, and my dad all love lamb chops, so every cookbook I do has to include a version for them. This one treats the meat simply, salting generously and searing it in a cast-iron skillet, griddle, or other heavy pan. Eating meat off the bone is fun any time of year, and I love to serve these lamb chops alongside an all-seasons accompaniment of white beans flavored with a generous dressing of Cilantro-Peanut Chutney (probably my favorite sauce in this book). I throw some pickled red onions on for a little sweet-tart hit of acidity—and because clearly I like them on just about everything.

— **MAKES 4 SERVINGS** —

¼ cup plus 3 tablespoons extra-virgin olive oil

2 garlic cloves, smashed

1 teaspoon toasted and cracked coriander seeds (see Toasting Nuts, Seeds, and Spices, page 199)

½ teaspoon sea salt, plus more to taste

12 lamb rib chops

One 15-ounce can cannellini beans, drained and rinsed

¼ cup Cilantro-Peanut Chutney (page 258)

Freshly cracked black pepper, to taste

½ cup Quick-Pickled Onions (page 246), to garnish

¼ cup fresh cilantro leaves, to garnish

2 tablespoons roasted peanuts, roughly chopped, to garnish

COMBINE ¼ cup of the olive oil, the garlic, coriander seeds, salt, and lamb chops in a large zip-top bag. Marinate at room temperature for 30 minutes or in the refrigerator up to overnight. If marinating in the refrigerator, be sure to let the lamb chops sit at room temperature for 30 minutes before cooking.

MEANWHILE, combine 1 tablespoon of the olive oil and the beans in a small saucepan over medium-low heat. Heat until just warmed through. Remove from the heat and toss with the Cilantro-Peanut Chutney. Cover the pan and keep warm.

WHEN ready to cook the lamb chops, heat a large heavy-bottomed pan over medium-high heat and add the remaining 2 tablespoons olive oil. Remove the lamb chops from the marinade and cook until golden brown on each side, about 3 minutes per side for medium-rare. (Discard the marinade.)

PLACE the beans on a platter and top with the lamb chops. Season with salt and pepper as desired. Garnish with the Quick-Pickled Onions, cilantro leaves, and chopped peanuts.

Branzino Stuffed with Red Onion, Lemon, and Oregano

Cooking branzino whole uses the bones and the skin to guarantee you the most delicious result, and stuffing it with shaved red onion, lemon slices, and oregano boosts flavor and moisture from the inside out. We normally just do this on the grill or a grill pan, since that little bit of char goes such a long way (you could roast it, too!). But if you feel like digging a hole on the beach, making a little bonfire, and grilling it al fresco, nothing is more mermaid-y than eating fresh seafood at the water's edge.

MAKES 6 SERVINGS

6 head-on branzino
(1 pound each), scaled and gutted

½ cup extra-virgin olive oil, plus more for garnish

Sea salt, to taste

2 small red onions, halved and thinly sliced

5 lemons, 3 thinly sliced into wheels and 2 cut into wedges for serving

1 bunch fresh oregano

20 scallions

Freshly cracked black pepper, to taste

RINSE the branzino and pat very dry. Season the inside of the cavities and both sides generously with olive oil and salt. Stuff the cavities with the red onion, lemon wheels, and oregano sprigs and drizzle with more olive oil.

TO COOK THE BRANZINO ON THE GRILL

HEAT the grill to high heat.

SCATTER the scallions perpendicular to the grill bars to create a bed for the branzino to lie on. This helps avoid sticking and makes flipping the fish much easier, and you get delicious charred scallions to serve with it. Some flames will jump up between the scallions to char bits of the fish skin as well.

PLACE the fish on top of the scallions and grill for about 8 minutes per side, flipping halfway through. When finished cooking, the fish will be juicy but firm, flaky, and opaque white to the bone.

TO ROAST THE BRANZINO IN THE OVEN

PREHEAT the oven to 425°F.

ARRANGE the scallions in a large roasting pan or sheet pan. Place the seasoned and stuffed fish on top of the scallions.

BAKE for 20 minutes, until the fish is firm, flaky, and opaque white to the bone.

SERVE the fish with lemon wedges and a fresh drizzle of olive oil. Season with additional salt and pepper if desired.

Spicy Slow-Cooker Chicken Chili with Black-Eyed Peas

Sometimes you just need to put a pot of chili on the stove and get ready to dig in to bold flavor and satisfying meaty goodness. This one is extra special because we're using chicken breast (honestly, most purists would probably call this *insanity*, but I kind of love pushing the boundary on what can taste decadent—I promise this will hit all the high notes), plus I make sure to add plenty of heat with smoky chipotle in adobo.

You can use any bean to stretch this wonderfully filling meal, but black-eyed peas feel like an extra dose of good luck and delicious flavor, so I always go for those. We make a big pot most Thursday evenings for a fun family chili dinner, and we have leftovers for quick and easy snacking or mealtimes throughout relaxed weekend days.

MAKES 6 SERVINGS

2 tablespoons extra-virgin olive oil (for the stovetop method)

1 pound boneless, skinless chicken breasts

1 small red onion, roughly chopped

1 poblano pepper, seeded and roughly chopped

2 garlic cloves, minced

1 tablespoon chili powder (3 tablespoons for the stovetop method)

2 teaspoons ground cumin

2 teaspoons dried oregano

1 chipotle in adobo, roughly chopped, plus 2 tablespoons adobo sauce (remove the seeds of the chile for milder heat)

1 tablespoon tomato paste

½ cup dry white wine or additional chicken stock if desired

1½ cups chicken stock or water (4½ cups chicken stock for the stovetop method)

Two 15-ounce cans fire-roasted diced tomatoes, drained of excess liquid

Two 15-ounce cans black-eyed peas, drained and rinsed

¼ cup prunes, roughly chopped

Sea salt and freshly cracked black pepper, to taste

TO SERVE (OPTIONAL)

Scallions, thinly sliced

Fresh cilantro

Hot sauce

Radishes, thinly sliced

Avocado, diced

TO MAKE THE CHILI IN A SLOW COOKER

IN a 6- to 8-quart slow cooker, combine the chicken breasts, red onion, poblano pepper, garlic, 1 tablespoon chili powder, the cumin, oregano, chipotle in adobo and sauce, tomato paste, white wine, 1½ cups chicken stock, tomatoes, black-eyed peas, and prunes, and season with ½ teaspoon salt. Stir well to combine.

COVER the slow cooker and cook on low for 7 to 8 hours or high for 4 hours, until the chicken is cooked through and the flavors have melded.

USE tongs to transfer the chicken breasts to a cutting board. Let rest for 10 minutes to allow the juices to reabsorb, then shred using two forks. Place the shredded chicken back into the slow cooker and stir to combine. Season again with salt and pepper as desired.

GARNISH with the toppings of your choice.

TO MAKE THE CHILI ON THE STOVETOP

HEAT the olive oil in a large heavy-bottomed pot or Dutch oven over medium-high heat. Cut the chicken breasts into 2-inch chunks and season on all sides with salt. Sear on all sides until golden but not cooked through, 5 to 6 minutes. Transfer to a plate.

ADD the onion, poblano pepper, and garlic to the pot and cook until softened, about 4 minutes. Add 3 tablespoons chili powder, the cumin, and the oregano and cook an additional minute. Add the chipotle in adobo plus sauce and tomato paste and cook a minute more. Season with salt.

DEGLAZE the pan with the wine, scraping up any browned bits on the bottom of the pot. Add 4 cups chicken stock, the chicken, tomatoes, black-eyed peas, and prunes. Bring to a boil and reduce to a simmer. Cover and simmer until the chicken is cooked through and easy to shred, about 15 minutes.

USE tongs to transfer the chicken chunks to a cutting board. Let rest for 10 minutes to allow the juices to reabsorb, then shred using two forks. Place the shredded chicken back into the pot and stir to combine. Continue simmering another 25 to 30 minutes, uncovered, to thicken and let the flavors meld, adding more stock or water if necessary.

GARNISH with the toppings of your choice.

on
the side

I KNOW TECHNICALLY SIDE DISHES ARE SUPPORTING ACTS,

but to me, they often steal the show. When we go out to dinner, I love making my meal out of a selection of sides so I get lots of little bites of many things—the more taste experiences, the merrier! It keeps your mouth guessing and is often the best way to make vegetables the star of any meal (keeping meat as a gorgeous complement rather than the centerpiece) without feeling like you've given anything up.

I wanted to celebrate sides in this book as a way you could think about preparing meals daily or keeping your fridge stocked with a variety of fresh, flavorful dishes, ready to pair with each other or just about anything else to round out a meal. Some real highlights (dare I say, sides that hustle?!) for me are BBQ Chicken Skewers; Sesame-Soy Smashed Cucumbers; Roasted Cauliflower with Scallions, Dates, and Hazelnuts; Zucchini-Scallion Baked Fritters; and the Meaty Greens Fried Rice.

MEDITERRANEAN CHICKEN SKEWERS 186

PEANUT-CHILI CHICKEN SKEWERS 188

BARBECUE CHICKEN SKEWERS 189

BRAISED BEETS AND GREENS WITH WALNUTS 190

ROASTED BROCCOLI RABE AND MILLET WITH CHERRIES 193

ZA'ATAR-ROASTED CARROTS AND
TURNIPS WITH GREMOLATA 194

STEAMED KABOCHA SQUASH WEDGES
WITH LIME MISO SAUCE 197

CAULIFLOWER RICE WITH CARAMELIZED
ONION AND HAZELNUTS 198

HARISSA SWEET POTATO AND SQUASH BAKE 200

COCONUT FORBIDDEN RICE 203

MEATY GREENS FRIED RICE 204

PARM-LESS EGGPLANT WITH SIMPLE TOMATO SAUCE 205

SESAME-SOY SMASHED CUCUMBERS 209

CRISPY ROASTED BUTTERNUT SQUASH AND
QUINOA WITH CURRANT VINAIGRETTE 210

ZUCCHINI-SCALLION BAKED FRITTERS 213

ROASTED CAULIFLOWER WITH
SCALLIONS, HAZELNUTS, AND DATES 214

Mediterranean Chicken Skewers

Chicken skewers are in heavy rotation around our house. It's easy to turn out a small mountain of them if you're always feeding a crowd like I am, and leftovers are amazing over any salad, chopped into casseroles, or eaten straight off the stick for a quick protein snack. This variation is my favorite, an easy blend of oregano, cumin, and garlic that pairs beautifully with just about everything, and the lemon juice keeps the skewers extra tender and juicy.

MAKES 4 SERVINGS

3 tablespoons extra-virgin olive oil

1 garlic clove, smashed

1 teaspoon dried oregano

1 teaspoon ground cumin

1 teaspoon cracked coriander seeds or ½ teaspoon ground coriander

½ teaspoon sweet paprika

Juice from 1 lemon (about 2 tablespoons)

¾ teaspoon fine sea salt, plus more to taste

1½ pounds boneless, skinless chicken thighs or breasts, cut into 1-inch chunks

Eight 10-inch wooden skewers, soaked in water

Freshly cracked black pepper, to taste

IN a large bowl, combine the olive oil, garlic, oregano, cumin, coriander seeds, paprika, lemon juice, and salt. Add the chicken, stir to coat, and let marinate for 30 minutes at room temperature.

PREHEAT a grill or grill pan to medium-high heat or preheat the oven to 375ºF. If using the oven, line a sheet pan with foil.

THREAD the chicken pieces onto the skewers, allowing any excess marinade to drip off.

IF using the grill, grill the skewers until the chicken is charred on both sides and cooked through, 5 to 6 minutes per side, until a meat thermometer registers 165ºF.

IF using the oven, place the marinated skewers on the prepared sheet pan and cook for 14 to 16 minutes, flipping the skewers halfway through, until the chicken is cooked through and a meat thermometer registers 165ºF.

SEASON with salt and pepper as desired and serve.

Peanut-Chili Chicken Skewers

My take on healthier chicken satay! I love how rich the peanut butter and coconut milk make these taste, while the tamari and sesame oil keep them wonderfully savory.

MAKES 4 SERVINGS

⅓ cup all-natural peanut butter

½ cup light coconut milk

1 tablespoon toasted sesame oil

2 tablespoons grapeseed oil

1 teaspoon Date Syrup (page 244)

1 teaspoon tamari or coconut aminos

Juice from 1 lime (about 2 tablespoons)

Pinch of crushed red chile flakes

½ teaspoon sea salt

1½ pounds boneless, skinless chicken thighs or breasts, cut into 1-inch chunks

Eight 10-inch wooden skewers, soaked in water

IN a large bowl, whisk together the peanut butter, coconut milk, sesame oil, grapeseed oil, Date Syrup, tamari, lime juice, chile flakes, and salt. Reserve ½ cup of the mixture in a separate bowl for brushing. Place the chicken chunks in the large bowl with the marinade and mix to coat. Marinate for 30 minutes at room temperature.

PREHEAT a grill or grill pan to medium-high heat or preheat the oven to 375ºF. If using the oven, line a sheet pan with foil.

THREAD the chicken onto the skewers, allowing any excess marinade to drip off (discard the marinade in the large bowl).

IF using the grill, grill the skewers until the chicken is charred on both sides and cooked through, 5 to 6 minutes per side, until a meat thermometer registers 165ºF.

IF using the oven, place the marinated skewers on the prepared sheet pan and cook for 14 to 16 minutes, flipping the skewers halfway through, until the chicken is cooked through and a meat thermometer registers 165ºF.

JUST before serving, use a clean brush to baste the chicken with the reserved marinade (or use a spoon to drizzle a bit over the tops). Enjoy.

Barbecue Chicken Skewers

Ah, barbecue chicken. Two words that mean pure smoky splendor. These skewers are a great way to get a taste of summer when you're craving it—any time of year, any night of the week. I especially love them with the Grilled Radicchio and Peach Salad on page 88.

—————————————— **MAKES 4 SERVINGS** ——————————————

1½ pounds boneless, skinless chicken thighs or breasts, cut into 1-inch chunks

Eight 10-inch wooden skewers, soaked in water

1 recipe Barbecue Sauce (page 261)

½ teaspoon sea salt, to taste

THREAD the chicken onto the wooden skewers. Divide the barbecue sauce in half. Brush half of the sauce over the chicken before cooking, taking care to coat all sides well. Season with salt.

PREHEAT a grill or grill pan to medium-high heat or preheat the oven to 375ºF. If using the oven, line a sheet pan with foil.

IF using the grill, grill the skewers until the chicken is charred on both sides and cooked through, 5 to 6 minutes per side, until a meat thermometer registers 165ºF.

IF using the oven, place the marinated skewers on the prepared sheet pan and cook for 14 to 16 minutes, flipping the skewers halfway through, until the chicken is cooked through and a meat thermometer registers 165ºF.

USE a clean brush to baste with the reserved sauce to finish.

Braised Beets and Greens with Walnuts

I have so many memories growing up of my mom with her fingers bright red from having peeled small mountains of roasted beets. They were a staple at our family dinner table, chopped and tossed with pinches of soft, creamy goat cheese and a sweet-tangy balsamic vinaigrette. The longer they sat, the more delicious they became as the dense meatiness of the beets drank up the surrounding liquid. This recipe speeds up the process with a quick braise in orange juice and stock, finished with a vibrant splash of apple cider vinegar.

I like to eat them on their own, hot or cold, or spooned over thick swishes of hummus with a sprinkle of walnuts for crunch.

───────────────── **MAKES 4 SERVINGS** ─────────────────

1 tablespoon extra-virgin olive oil

2 pounds medium beets, trimmed, peeled, and cut into ½-inch-thick wedges, greens reserved

½ red onion, thinly sliced

2 garlic cloves, minced

1 tablespoon fresh thyme leaves

½ teaspoon sea salt, plus more to taste

Juice from 1 orange plus 1 teaspoon of zest (zest optional)

2 cups vegetable stock

2 tablespoons apple cider vinegar

Freshly cracked black pepper, to taste

½ cup walnuts, toasted and chopped (see Toasting Nuts, Seeds, and Spices, page 199), to garnish

¼ cup fresh basil leaves, torn, to garnish

HEAT the olive oil in a medium pot or saucepan over medium-high heat. Add the beets and cook until slightly softened, about 4 minutes. Add the onion, garlic, thyme, and salt, and cook another minute. Add the orange juice, zest (if using), and vegetable stock. Bring to a boil and reduce to a simmer. Partially cover the pot and let the beets braise until tender, 15 to 18 minutes.

MEANWHILE, wash and roughly chop the beet greens. When the beets are tender, stir in the greens, allowing them to wilt. Add the apple cider vinegar and stir to combine. Simmer for another 2 or 3 minutes. Season with salt and pepper if needed.

REMOVE from the heat and garnish with the chopped walnuts and torn basil.

SERVE alone or over any of the hummus selections starting on page 236.

NOTE. If you don't have oranges, you can substitute ¼ cup of water, red wine, or even apple juice in this recipe.

Roasted Broccoli Rabe and Millet with Cherries

This recipe is simply delicious and can accommodate a variety of different seasonal fruits to be enjoyed year-round—if you can't find cherries, pit and slice any ripe stone fruit. I especially love the natural sweet-tart flavor of plums. The cherries blister and wilt ever so slightly as they warm in the pan with the shallots, adding even more flavor to the dressing that coats the golden-brown roasted broccoli. A few choice dollops of goat cheese give the sensation of decadence without being overwhelming. You can leave the cheese off if you prefer, but I find its cool tanginess really binds all the elements together beautifully.

─────────────────── **MAKE 4 SERVINGS** ───────────────────

1½ pounds broccoli rabe, cut into long florets

3 tablespoons extra-virgin olive oil

¾ teaspoon sea salt, plus more to taste

1 cup millet

1 shallot, minced

1 cup pitted and halved cherries or grapes

1 teaspoon ground cumin

1 tablespoon chopped fresh oregano or 1 teaspoon dried oregano

Freshly cracked black pepper, to taste

½ cup crumbled goat cheese

Juice from 1 lemon (about 2 tablespoons), plus 1 teaspoon lemon zest (optional)

1 tablespoon finely chopped fresh mint, to garnish

PREHEAT the oven to 400ºF.

TOSS the broccoli rabe with 2 tablespoons of the olive oil and ½ teaspoon of the salt in a large bowl. Spread evenly on a sheet pan and roast for 25 to 30 minutes, until the broccoli is lightly golden, flipping halfway through.

MEANWHILE, cook the millet according to the package instructions.

HEAT the remaining 1 tablespoon olive oil in a small sauté pan and add the shallot and the remaining ¼ teaspoon salt. Cook until softened, adding the cherries, cumin, and oregano during the last minute of cooking, gently stirring to combine but taking care not to break apart the cherries too much. Toss the cherry mixture with the warm cooked millet and season with salt and pepper.

TO serve, spread the millet onto a large platter and top with the roasted broccoli, goat cheese, and lemon juice and zest (if using). Scatter with fresh mint and serve.

Za'atar-Roasted Carrots and Turnips with Gremolata

This preparation works equally well whether you want to use the suggested za'atar—a lemony, herbal spice mix with cumin, sumac, Aleppo pepper, and sesame seeds, among other spices—or a simple store-bought curry powder. The point is that sweet root vegetables get only sweeter when you roast them, and they condense into their meatiest form, which can really stand up to bold, strong spice flavors. I love to layer these over a pillow of thick, tangy yogurt that will catch any delicious escaping juices, and the gremolata lightens the whole bowl with its citrus and herb freshness.

——————— **MAKES 4 SERVINGS** ———————

1 pound whole baby carrots, or large carrots peeled and sliced in half lengthwise

1 large turnip or 2 small turnips, peeled and cut into ½-inch-thick wedges

2 tablespoons extra-virgin olive oil

½ teaspoon sea salt, plus more to taste

2 teaspoons za'atar

Freshly cracked black pepper, to taste

2 tablespoons golden raisins

1 tablespoon Parsley and Mint Gremolata (page 255)

PREHEAT the oven to 400°F and line a sheet pan with parchment paper.

TOSS the carrots and turnips with the olive oil and salt in a large bowl. Spread evenly on the prepared sheet pan and roast for 20 to 25 minutes, until golden and tender, flipping halfway through.

SET aside to cool for 5 minutes. Toss with the za'atar and season with salt and pepper if needed. Transfer to a platter, sprinkle with the raisins, and spoon Parsley and Mint Gremolata over the top.

Steamed Kabocha Squash Wedges
with Lime Miso Sauce

Kabocha squash looks like Cinderella's carriage and is utterly delectable: sweeter than pumpkin, lighter than sweet potato, less watery than butternut squash—I really can't rave enough. For this recipe, we're going to steam it, a wonderful cooking process that lets us keep as much nutrition in our food as possible rather than rinsing those vitamins down the drain with the cooking water. The squash is hydrated and delicately soft—a perfect mate for slightly sweet, a-little-bit-funky Lime Miso Sauce and a generous drizzle of Chili Sesame Oil, which I know you'll love and use on everything after you make it once! Fried garlic, chile flakes, and sesame seeds are better than a perfect pair, because there are three of them.

MAKES 4 SERVINGS

One 3-pound kabocha squash, scrubbed, seeded, and cut into 1½-inch-thick wedges

¼ cup Lime Miso Sauce (page 260), to garnish

1 tablespoon Chili Sesame Oil (page 253), to garnish

PLACE a steamer basket in the bottom of a pot and fill the pot with 2 inches of water. Bring to a boil over medium-high heat. Add the squash wedges, cover the pot with a lid, and steam for 10 to 15 minutes, until the squash is tender when pierced with the tip of a knife.

ARRANGE the squash on a platter and drizzle with the Lime Miso Sauce and Chili Sesame Oil.

Cauliflower Rice with Caramelized Onion and Hazelnuts

Cauliflower rice, you versatile, low-carb vegetable in disguise! You're a saucy minx, sidling up to every rice preparation in town, hoodwinking us with your neutrality, beckoning us to eat the whole bowl! Okay, fine! I'll do it!

While cauliflower rice is indeed a great gift to the world of lightened-up cooking, this dish is really all about the caramelized onions. There are also hazelnuts . . . chile flakes . . . and anchovies. I almost didn't tell you about the anchovies; I'd rather have you taste this dish and *then* find out there are anchovies in it. But alas, you're cooking it for yourself, so there's no hiding them. Be bold, and dive in. Delicious.

MAKES 4 SERVINGS

¼ cup extra-virgin olive oil

2 medium yellow onions, thinly sliced

1 teaspoon sea salt, plus more to taste

1 cauliflower head, cut into florets, or 8 cups frozen cauliflower rice

2 garlic cloves, minced

2 anchovies, mashed

¼ teaspoon crushed red chile flakes

¼ cup blanched hazelnuts, toasted (see Toasting Nuts, Seeds, and Spices, opposite) and chopped

Freshly ground black pepper, to taste

¼ cup chopped fresh parsley leaves and stems, to garnish

HEAT 2 tablespoons of the olive oil in a large sauté pan over medium-low heat. Add the onions, season with the salt, and cook, stirring regularly, until they develop a deep, rich brown color with no burning. To achieve consistency and maximum concentration of flavor, cook the onions for at least 15 minutes until golden and ideally 30 to 45 minutes until deeply golden. Consider making extra if you're already doing this step, because you can freeze leftover caramelized onions and use them on everything.

MEANWHILE, in the bowl of a food processor fitted with the blade attachment, add the cauliflower and pulse until it resembles rice. Alternatively, you can grate the cauliflower on the large holes of a box grater. Transfer the riced cauliflower to a bowl and set aside.

ADD the garlic, anchovies, and chile flakes to the caramelized onions and cook another minute, until the anchovies have melted. Increase the heat to medium-high and add the remaining 2 tablespoons olive oil and the cauliflower rice. Stir to combine and cook for 3 to 4 minutes, until just tender. Add the hazelnuts, season with additional salt and pepper if needed, and serve scattered with the fresh parsley.

TOASTING NUTS: STOVETOP METHOD

Place nuts in an even layer in a nonstick or stainless steel sauté pan over medium-low heat. Toast for 3 to 6 minutes, until fragrant, nutty, and golden, swirling the pan regularly to ensure even cooking and avoid burning. Transfer to a plate or clean dish towel to cool completely.

Smaller nuts like slivered almonds and pine nuts will have the shortest toasting time. More tender nuts that are less dense, like walnuts, pecans, and pistachios, will cook a minute or two faster than denser nuts like almonds and hazelnuts.

TOASTING NUTS: OVEN METHOD

The oven provides a very easy and more even toasting method. Preheat it to 350ºF and place the nuts on a sheet pan. Toast for 5 to 10 minutes, shaking the pan every few minutes. Toast until they are fragrant and golden (or one shade darker, depending on the nut). Check every few minutes for a nice, toasty smell and to ensure no nuts are burning. Transfer to a plate or clean dish towel to cool completely.

TOASTING SEEDS: STOVETOP METHOD

Place the seeds in an even layer in a nonstick or stainless steel sauté pan over medium-low heat. Toast for 3 to 6 minutes, swirling and shaking the pan often for even toasting and to avoid burning. Toast seeds of similar size at the same time for even cooking. Transfer to a plate to cool completely.

TOASTING SEEDS: OVEN METHOD

Preheat the oven to 350ºF and place the seeds in an even layer on a sheet pan. Toast for 5 to 10 minutes, shaking the pan every few minutes for even cooking. Watch for the seeds to turn golden and fragrant, then transfer to a plate to cool completely.

TOASTING SPICES

Place whole spices in a small nonstick or stainless steel sauté pan over medium-low heat. Let toast until fragrant, 2 to 5 minutes, swirling and shaking the pan frequently for even toasting and to avoid burning. Some spices may turn a shade darker; you should be able to smell the oils blooming. Heat whole spices of similar size together for even toasting. Transfer to a plate to cool.

GRINDING SPICES

When the spices are cooled, place them in a mortar and pestle and grind until they are broken into pieces or use a flat, heavy-bottomed skillet to gently crush them against a cutting board. This will give you cracked spices (a coarser grind). For finely ground spices, continue grinding in the mortar and pestle or place in an electric spice grinder and grind into powder. To finely grind larger quantities, use a high-speed blender.

TOASTING NUTS, SEEDS, AND SPICES

Harissa Sweet Potato and Squash Bake

A beguiling combination of hot and smoky chiles, spices, herbs, and garlic, harissa is a frequent friend of mine. I spread it on avocado toast in *Relish*, roasted it with carrots in *The Happy Cook*, and now am adding it to a warm bath of coconut milk to simmer with thin slices of butternut squash and sweet potatoes as they soften into melting oblivion. Is this my favorite harissa creation to date? Let's make some and discuss.

————————————————**MAKES 6 TO 8 SERVINGS**————————————————

1 tablespoon plus 2 teaspoons extra-virgin olive oil

One 13.5-ounce can light coconut milk, well shaken

¼ cup tapioca flour

2 garlic cloves, minced

1 teaspoon ground coriander

¾ teaspoon sea salt, plus more to taste

2 to 3 teaspoons harissa paste (such as DEA or Mina)

1 medium butternut squash, peeled and seeded

Two large sweet potatoes, peeled

3 tablespoons Crunchy Dukkah (page 256), to garnish

PREHEAT the oven to 375°F. Grease a 7 x 11-inch baking dish with 2 teaspoons of the olive oil.

PLACE ¼ cup of the coconut milk in a small bowl and gradually whisk in the tapioca flour to make a slurry. It should look almost like glue. Set aside.

IN a medium saucepan, heat the remaining 1 tablespoon olive oil over medium heat. Add the garlic, coriander, and salt and cook until fragrant, about 30 seconds. Add the remaining coconut milk from the can and whisk to combine. Let warm through until steaming but not simmering, a minute or so.

DRIZZLE in the slurry and cook, whisking constantly as the mixture simmers and thickens to the consistency of pudding (this may seem super thick, but the vegetables will release a lot of water while baking). Stir in the harissa, remove the pan from the heat, and set aside. Cut the butternut squash and sweet potato into ⅛-inch-thick slices on a mandoline while the coconut mixture cools and place them in a large bowl. Pour the coconut milk mixture over the squash and sweet potatoes and toss to evenly coat (using hands is helpful here!).

SPREAD evenly in the prepared baking dish. Cover with foil and bake for 40 minutes, then remove the foil and bake until the vegetables are bubbling and tender when pierced with the tip of a knife, 20 to 30 more minutes.

IF a golden brown and crunchy top is desired, preheat the broiler. Broil for 3 to 5 minutes, until golden.

LET cool for 10 to 15 minutes. Garnish with the Crunchy Dukkah and serve.

Coconut Forbidden Rice

Equal parts sweet and savory, this rice steams in a mix of water and coconut milk, so it is rich and flavorful without being overly fatty. I love adding the savory elements of scallions and garlic at the start so they can perfume the entire cooking process, then topping the finished rice with toasty sesame seeds.

——————— **MAKES 4 SERVINGS** ———————

1 tablespoon coconut oil

2 scallions, white and light green parts only, minced

2 garlic cloves, minced

1 cup black forbidden rice, rinsed

1 cup full-fat coconut milk

1 tablespoon Date Syrup (page 244)

½ teaspoon sea salt

1 tablespoon toasted sesame seeds (see Toasting Nuts, Seeds, and Spices, page 199), to garnish

1 Fresno chile, thinly sliced, to garnish

HEAT the coconut oil in a medium saucepan over medium-high heat. Add the scallions and garlic and cook for 2 minutes. Add the rice and toast for 1 to 2 minutes. Add 2 cups water, the coconut milk, Date Syrup, and salt. Bring to a boil, then reduce to a simmer and cook, uncovered, for 30 minutes, stirring frequently (add more water if needed). Fluff the cooked rice with a fork.

GARNISH with the sesame seeds and Fresno chile and serve.

Meaty Greens Fried Rice

This dish was inspired by a simple mash of brown rice, sauteed onion, and spinach I make for my toddlers all the time. It's so good that I always find myself hoping for leftovers. I'd sometimes add ground turkey or chicken and an egg, and then soy sauce, and it basically became fried rice. Nothing like the authentic version, every bit as delicious, and an amazing way to use up leftover rice. If you want to leave the meat out, feel free to add beans instead. Pinto would work nicely.

———————————————— **MAKES 4 SERVINGS** ————————————————

3 tablespoons coconut oil

1 small yellow onion, finely chopped

4 scallions, thinly sliced, white and light green parts separated from dark green

2 garlic cloves, minced

1 pound ground chicken

2 cups finely chopped stemmed leafy greens (such as kale, spinach, or chard)

4 large eggs

¼ cup tamari or coconut aminos, plus more to taste

1 tablespoon toasted sesame oil

1 cup fresh or thawed frozen peas

2 cups cooked brown rice, preferably a day old or spread out and dried on the counter while you prepare the rest of the dish (or try quinoa, millet, or even frozen cauliflower rice!)

1 serrano pepper, thinly sliced, to garnish

Chili Sesame Oil (page 253), to garnish (optional)

Sea salt and freshly cracked black pepper, to taste

HEAT the coconut oil in a large nonstick sauté pan over medium-high heat. Add the onion, dark green scallions, and garlic and cook until softened, 3 to 4 minutes. Add the chicken and use a wooden spoon or spatula to break it apart as it browns, 7 to 9 minutes. Add the greens, stir to combine, and cook so most of their liquid evaporates but they are still bright green, about 3 minutes.

WHISK the eggs, tamari, and sesame oil in a medium bowl. Make a well in the center of the chicken mixture, add the egg mixture, and reduce the heat to medium-low. Gently scramble the eggs using a rubber spatula until small curds begin to form, about a minute. Add the peas and brown rice and toss together with the chicken mixture and the eggs to heat through and finish cooking. Resist the urge to stir too often so your rice crisps up a bit and doesn't stick together.

TRANSFER to a serving plate and adorn with the white and light green scallions, serrano pepper slices, a drizzle of Chili Sesame Oil (if using), and tamari, salt, and pepper to taste.

Parm-less Eggplant with Simple Tomato Sauce

I have family in Staten Island, so trust me, I know about delicious eggplant parmesan! But if we're being honest, the traditional recipes are more about sauce, bread, and cheese than veg—and there's a time and a place for that! This version elevates the eggplant by giving it an extra-crispy coating in rice flour, a sprinkle with the king of salty cheeses (Pecorino Romano!), a smattering of herbs, a splash of simple tomato sauce, and a few chile flakes for good measure.

———————————————————— **MAKES 4 SERVINGS** ————————————————————

FRIED EGGPLANT

1 medium globe eggplant (about 1 pound), sliced into ½-inch-thick rounds

1¼ teaspoons sea salt, plus more to taste

1 cup rice flour

¼ cup grated Pecorino Romano

½ teaspoon dried oregano

1 teaspoon fresh thyme leaves

½ teaspoon garlic powder

¼ cup extra-virgin olive oil, plus more as needed

Freshly cracked black pepper, to taste

SIMPLE TOMATO SAUCE

2 tablespoons extra-virgin olive oil

1 small yellow onion, finely chopped

2 garlic cloves, minced

½ teaspoon dried oregano

½ teaspoon sea salt, plus more to taste

¼ cup tomato paste

One 28-ounce can crushed tomatoes

Freshly cracked black pepper, to taste

TO SERVE

½ cup grated Pecorino Romano

2 tablespoons chopped fresh parsley

2 tablespoons chopped fresh basil leaves

Pinch of crushed red chile flakes (optional)

PLACE a baking rack in a sheet pan. Sprinkle the eggplant slices on both sides with 1 teaspoon of the salt. Place on the prepared baking rack and let sit for 15 minutes (this will draw excess moisture out of the eggplant).

MEANWHILE, make the simple tomato sauce. Heat the olive oil in a medium pot over medium-high heat. Add the onion and sauté, stirring occasionally, until softened, 4 to 5 minutes. Add the garlic, oregano, and salt and cook another minute. Add the tomato paste, crushed tomatoes, and ½ cup water and bring to a boil. Once boiling, lower to a simmer for 20 minutes, stirring regularly. Add water a couple of tablespoons at a time if the sauce becomes too thick, and return it to a simmer. Taste and season with salt and pepper as desired. Remove from the heat and reserve until ready to use.

(recipe continues)

LINE a plate with paper towels. In a large shallow bowl, whisk the rice flour, Pecorino Romano, oregano, thyme, garlic powder, and the remaining ¼ teaspoon salt. Add ½ cup water and whisk until a smooth batter forms (a little thicker than pancake batter).

IN a large cast-iron skillet over medium-high heat, heat the olive oil until shimmering. Pat the eggplant dry on both sides with paper towels. Dip the eggplant slices into the rice flour batter, allowing any excess to drip off. Place in the hot oil and shallow fry on both sides until golden brown, 4 to 5 minutes per side. Transfer to the prepared plate and immediately season with a pinch each of salt and pepper. Repeat with the remaining eggplant slices, adding more oil if needed and taking care that the oil doesn't get too hot or that too many burned pieces don't collect and turn it bitter. If this happens, empty the olive oil into a small bowl to cool before discarding it, wipe down the pan, add fresh oil to the pan, and continue.

SPOON some of the tomato sauce into four shallow bowls and top with a few eggplant slices. Garnish with a sprinkle of Pecorino Romano, parsley, basil, and chile flakes (if using).

Sesame-Soy Smashed Cucumbers

I could eat bowls and bowls of this stuff. What I mean to say is, I *do* eat bowls and bowls of this stuff. In fact, I had to figure out how to make this recipe because, previously, I could find smashed cucumbers made the way I like only at an always-packed ramen restaurant near our old apartment in NYC. John and I would head there whenever we could sneak in dinner alone (the hour-plus wait at the bar made it less than ideal to bring the kids). When this dish finally arrived at our table, it would be as one single, perfect cucumber, and I would try to savor it but I was also so gleeful at the flavor explosion happening in my mouth that it would always be over too soon. Not anymore!

Now I make this recipe, if not daily, then at least several times a week. For the perfect snack to chase away sweet cravings in the afternoon. As something to pick on while I make dinner. Smashing the cucumbers breaks them open to drink up the dressing of toasted sesame oil, rice vinegar, and tamari, with just a splash of sweet Date Syrup. They are cool, crunchy, and bursting with juicy flavor, and I think it's fair to say: neither I, nor the cucumber, has ever had it so good.

--- **MAKES 4 SERVINGS** ---

2 pounds Persian cucumbers

1 teaspoon sea salt

1 tablespoon toasted sesame oil

1 tablespoon grapeseed oil

2 teaspoons rice vinegar

2 teaspoons tamari or coconut aminos

1 teaspoon Date Syrup (page 244)

1 garlic clove, minced

2 teaspoons toasted sesame seeds (see Toasting Nuts, Seeds, and Spices, page 199), to garnish

Chili Sesame Oil (page 253), to garnish

PLACE the cucumbers on a cutting board and use the flat side of a chef's knife and little hits with the heel of your hand or a rolling pin to lightly smash the vegetable and gently burst the skin in places. Cut the cucumbers on the bias into 2-inch pieces. Toss the pieces with the salt and place in a strainer over the sink for 10 to 15 minutes to drain the excess liquid.

MEANWHILE, in a large bowl, whisk together the sesame oil, grapeseed oil, rice vinegar, tamari, Date Syrup, and garlic.

TOSS the cucumbers in the strainer to release any more excess liquid and add them to the bowl with the dressing. Gently toss to coat. Garnish with the toasted sesame seeds and a drizzle of Chili Sesame Oil.

NOTE. If you don't have the Chili Sesame Oil available, just add ¼ teaspoon of chile flakes and ½ tablespoon of toasted sesame seeds to this recipe for some welcome heat and nutty flavor.

Crispy Roasted Butternut Squash and Quinoa with Currant Vinaigrette

This is a colorful salad that I would say has about a 50:50 ratio of quinoa to everything else, which in my book is just right. I want the quinoa to be there to play with everything and fill me up, but then I kind of want it to fade into the background and let the more flavorful, exciting elements like nicely spiced and golden-brown roasted cubes of butternut squash, plenty of pulled fresh parsley and scallions, and the excellently acidic currant vinaigrette steal the show.

MAKES 4 TO 6 SERVINGS

BUTTERNUT SQUASH

½ teaspoon chili powder

1 teaspoon ground cumin

1 teaspoon dried oregano

Sea salt, to taste

2 cups cubed butternut squash (1-inch cubes)

¼ cup extra-virgin olive oil

QUINOA

1 cup quinoa

1½ cups water or broth

½ teaspoon sea salt

One 15-ounce can chickpeas, drained and rinsed

½ cup fresh parsley leaves, torn

4 scallions, thinly sliced

1 recipe Currant Vinaigrette (page 279)

PREHEAT the oven to 350°F.

TO make the butternut squash, combine the chili powder, cumin, oregano, and a pinch of salt in a small bowl. Place the squash on a sheet pan in an even layer. Drizzle with the olive oil and sprinkle with the spice mixture. Toss to evenly coat the squash. Roast for 45 minutes, flipping halfway through, or until golden brown and tender.

MEANWHILE, make the quinoa. Rinse the quinoa in a fine-mesh sieve until the water runs clear, about 2 minutes. Transfer the quinoa to a medium saucepan over medium heat and toast until it smells nutty, about 2 minutes. Add the water and salt and bring to a boil, then reduce to a simmer. Cover and cook according to the package instructions. Once the liquid has evaporated, remove from the heat, cover the pot with a paper towel, and place the lid back on top. The paper towel absorbs any excess liquid, allowing the quinoa to steam perfectly as it rests. Let it sit and steam for 5 minutes, then fluff with two forks.

IN a large bowl, combine the quinoa, chickpeas, parsley, and scallions with enough Currant Vinaigrette to coat and toss to combine. Arrange on a serving platter and pile with little handfuls of squash on top.

Zucchini-Scallion Baked Fritters

Ohhh, these are dangerous. In a good way. Actually, in a *great* way, since they're mainly vegetable and held together with just a bit of almond flour and egg. Light and tender, fluffy but hearty enough to withstand a drag through garlicky tzatziki, they're the perfect pillowy nibble to accompany everything from roast fish to grilled chicken to a nice, hearty salad.

MAKES 4 SERVINGS

Pure extra-virgin olive oil spray

2½ cups shredded zucchini, from 1 to 2 medium zucchini

½ small yellow onion, grated

1 garlic clove, grated

1 large egg, separated, plus 1 egg white

⅓ cup almond flour

2 tablespoons chopped dill, plus more for garnish

½ teaspoon sea salt, plus more to taste

3 scallions, thinly sliced

Freshly cracked black pepper, to taste

¼ cup Herbed Yogurt Dip (page 257)

PREHEAT the oven to 400°F. Line two sheet pans with parchment paper. Grease the parchment paper with the olive oil spray. Place the zucchini in a clean kitchen towel and wring out any excess moisture.

IN a large bowl, combine the zucchini, onion, garlic, egg yolk, almond flour, dill, salt, and half the scallions. Beat the egg whites with a whisk in a medium bowl until frothy. Gently fold the egg whites into the zucchini mixture until light and combined.

SCOOP 2 heaping tablespoons of the zucchini mixture onto the prepared sheet pan and lightly press to flatten. Repeat to form 10 fritters total. Spray the tops of the fritters with olive oil. Bake for 10 minutes, flip, then bake for another 10 minutes, until golden brown and crispy on the edges. Remove from the oven and season with salt and pepper.

SPREAD the Herbed Yogurt Dip on the bottom of four bowls. Top each bowl with 2 or 3 zucchini fritters and a scattering of the remaining scallions and dill and serve.

NOTE. If you need these fritters in a hurry, they are truly excellent pan-fried. This is obviously a more decadent take, but just wanted to let you know in case you are ever in need.

Roasted Cauliflower with Scallions, Hazelnuts, and Dates

Stop whatever you are doing and immediately decide that tonight you are making this lusciously golden roasted cauliflower, topped with my favorite-ever sweet-plus-savory, highly addictive mix of gently melting dates, sizzling scallions, and crunchy hazelnuts. I do sometimes like to sneak in capers and just two anchovies for a little salty wink, but both are optional if you want to stick to my original recipe. Okay. Make it. Send me a picture before you devour. Confirm for me that this is, in fact, the best possible combination of flavors on a vegetable imaginable. I will agree. I will probably then have to make it for myself thanks to the then implanted craving I will have. We will both have lovely evenings.

MAKES 4 SERVINGS

1 medium cauliflower head, excess core removed, cut or broken into 8 wedges

2 tablespoons extra-virgin olive oil or avocado oil

½ teaspoon sea salt, plus more to taste

1 lemon, thinly sliced into rounds

1 bunch scallions, finely chopped

2 garlic cloves, minced

2 anchovies, roughly chopped (optional)

¼ cup capers, drained and chopped (optional)

4 Medjool dates, pitted and roughly chopped (or ¼ cup golden raisins)

½ cup roasted hazelnuts (see Toasting Nuts, Seeds, and Spices, page 199), roughly chopped

¼ cup roughly chopped fresh parsley, to garnish

Freshly cracked black pepper, to taste

PREHEAT the oven to 425ºF. Place a sheet pan in the oven to preheat.

PLACE the cauliflower in a large bowl and toss with 1 tablespoon of the oil and the salt. Carefully remove the hot sheet pan from the oven and add the cauliflower wedges. Scatter the lemon slices around the cauliflower in a single layer. Roast until the cauliflower is golden brown, crispy on the edges, and almost tender at the stalk, about 30 minutes. The lemons will concentrate their flavor and be charred in places.

MEANWHILE, place a medium sauté pan over medium heat and add the remaining tablespoon of oil. Add the scallions and a pinch of salt and cook until softened, 2 minutes. Add the garlic and anchovies (if using) and cook another minute to melt the anchovies, using a wooden spoon to help. Add the capers (if using) and dates and cook another minute, so the dates begin to caramelize and soften as they warm. Add the chopped hazelnuts and stir just to combine. Taste for seasoning.

ARRANGE the roasted cauliflower on a serving platter and scatter the date and hazelnut mixture over the top. Finish with the fresh parsley and a few cracks of pepper.

snacks
and savory
bites

ESPECIALLY WHEN I'M TRYING TO RESET MY SYSTEM,

find my happy weight, and break bad habits that we all fall prey to when life gets extra busy/stressful/exciting/fun, I've learned how important it is that I eat *enough* at mealtimes so I'm not hungry during the hours in between. Whether with protein, fat, fiber, healthy carbs, or all of the above, eating well should still feel indulgent, delicious, memorable—and filling!

My goal is to avoid the need to mindlessly graze throughout the day, but I'm also a pragmatist. I know that by staying prepared, I set myself up for success. That's when I turn to this chapter!

These snacks can be made ahead and brought along for the ride (and what a wild ride it is!). Nori Popcorn is not to be missed! Italian Roasted Chickpeas, Most Addictive Kale Chips, and pretty pink Beet Hummus are some other fan favorites around these parts.

CHILI-GARLIC JAPANESE YAM CUBES   220

SWEET AND SPICY PECANS WITH
CHIPOTLE AND CUMIN   223

ROSEMARY, THYME, AND CINNAMON NUT MIX   224

MIXED OLIVE TAPENADE   225

NORI POPCORN   227

LEMON-FENNEL GINGER TEA   228

THE MOST ADDICTIVE KALE CHIPS   230

EASY SEEDED CRACKER BARK   231

ITALIAN ROASTED CHICKPEAS   232

SMOKED EGGPLANT DIP   235

CLASSIC HUMMUS   236

BEET HUMMUS   238

GREEN HUMMUS   239

Chili-Garlic Japanese Yam Cubes

Japanese yams are truly nature's candy. Every bit as sweet—maybe sweeter, actually?—as their orange counterparts, but with a creamy white flesh that feels denser, creamier, and even more luscious. If you roast them whole, you'll discover a flavor very close to vanilla-scented pudding evolves as the sugars caramelize and the potato softens. Delicious. But when you cube the yams, toss them with a bit of olive oil and spices, and roast away, then crisp, sweet plus savory, fiber-packed, totally snackable heaven awaits!

MAKES 4 SERVINGS

---

2 Japanese yams (a little over 1 pound), peeled and cut into ½-inch cubes

2 tablespoons extra-virgin olive oil

½ teaspoon ground cumin

½ teaspoon dried oregano

¼ teaspoon crushed red chile flakes

1 teaspoon garlic salt

PREHEAT the oven to 425°F.

TOSS the yams, olive oil, cumin, oregano, chile flakes, and garlic salt in a large bowl. Transfer to a sheet pan and roast for 25 to 30 minutes, flipping halfway through, until golden brown and crunchy. Serve warm or let cool completely, then store in an airtight container in the refrigerator for up to 3 days. They can quickly be reheated at 325°F until nicely crisp again.

Sweet and Spicy Pecans with Chipotle and Cumin

These are particularly lovely at the end of a meal or for a quick afternoon pick-me-up with tea or coffee. Pecans are so meaty, and I love how they take on rich, smoky chipotle heat and a tiny hit of coconut sugar to enhance their delicate buttery notes. Though they are optional, the nigella seeds (also known as black onion seeds) are really something special—they provide such a gloriously addictive savory moment that feels unexpected paired with the earthy, spicy, sweetness of all the other seasonings. They can be hard to find at the grocery store, so they are definitely optional! I order mine online by the pound—once you start that habit, it's hard to stop.

MAKES 8 SERVINGS

1 egg white

3 tablespoons coconut sugar

1 teaspoon chipotle chile powder

1 teaspoon cumin seeds

2 teaspoons nigella seeds (optional)

Pinch of cayenne pepper

½ teaspoon sea salt

2 cups raw pecans

PREHEAT the oven to 300°F. Line a sheet pan with parchment paper.

IN a medium bowl, whisk the egg white with 1 tablespoon water until pale and foamy. Add the coconut sugar, chipotle chile powder, cumin seeds, nigella seeds (if using), cayenne, and salt and whisk to combine. Add the pecans and toss to coat. Spread evenly on the prepared sheet pan.

ROAST for 25 to 30 minutes, stirring every 10 minutes or so to keep the nuts from burning or sticking to each other. They should be a caramelized and deep golden brown and smell richly toasty. They will continue to crisp as they cool. I like to let the nuts cool on the pan and use a wooden spoon or spatula to break any clusters apart so you get nice, individual pieces. Store in an airtight container for up to 1 week.

Rosemary, Thyme, and Cinnamon Nut Mix

Nuts do pack a bit of fat, but it's good, healthy fat your body understands and knows how to harness to fuel long-term energy and satiety. Adding the savory hit of fresh herbs and sweet cinnamon keeps every bite interesting and satisfying enough that a little goes a long way.

MAKES 8 SERVINGS

2 cups mixed raw nuts (almonds, cashews, walnuts, pecans, hazelnuts, and pistachios work well!)

1 tablespoon fresh thyme leaves

1 tablespoon finely chopped fresh rosemary leaves

½ teaspoon ground cinnamon

½ teaspoon onion powder

3 tablespoons extra-virgin olive oil

¼ to ½ teaspoon sea salt, to taste

PREHEAT the oven to 325°F.

COMBINE the nuts, thyme, rosemary, cinnamon, onion powder, olive oil, and salt in a medium bowl and toss until coated. Spread evenly on a sheet pan.

ROAST for 15 to 18 minutes, tossing halfway through, until fragrant and golden.

SERVE warm or at room temperature. Store in an airtight container for up to 1 week.

Mixed Olive Tapenade

My daughter Philomena is the reason olive tapenade is a constant presence in our home. From the time she was one, she had me pitting and chopping every sort of olive for it—the saltier the better. I eventually started making this delicious pureed olive spread to have her favorite spoonful ready at mealtime, and it quickly became one of my favorite sandwich toppers and vegetable accompaniments. A little goes a long way to bring big flavor to dips, spreads, and even soups and chilis!

───────────────── **MAKES 4 SERVINGS** ─────────────────

1 cup pitted kalamata olives

½ cup pitted oil-cured black olives

2 garlic cloves

2 tablespoons capers, drained

1 teaspoon dried oregano

2 anchovy fillets

¼ cup extra-virgin olive oil

Sea salt and freshly cracked black pepper, to taste

IN the bowl of a food processor fitted with the blade attachment, combine the olives, garlic, capers, oregano, and anchovies. Pulse a few times to break down, then add the olive oil and puree until a fine but textured paste forms, scraping down the sides as needed. Season with salt and pepper.

ENJOY immediately with fresh cut veggies or Easy Seeded Cracker Bark (page 231). Store in a small airtight container and refrigerate for up to 1 month.

Nori Popcorn

Nori is a sea vegetable (seaweed) that's loaded with essential minerals, including iodine—critical for thyroid function, healthy metabolism, and cell repair all over the body! Most important for this recipe, nori adds the most delicious salty, savory flavor to always-delicious popcorn. I love to air-pop the golden corn kernels (I've also given you a stovetop method, just in case) and then use a spray bottle to lightly mist a little oil to help the coating stick into every nook and cranny. Grab a handful!

MAKES 15 CUPS

2 sheets nori

½ teaspoon crushed red chile flakes (optional)

2 tablespoons toasted sesame seeds (see Toasting Nuts, Seeds, and Spices, page 199)

Sea salt, to taste

2 tablespoons avocado oil, olive oil, or grapeseed oil

½ cup popcorn kernels

OPTIONAL TO TOAST THE NORI: If working with a gas stovetop, turn your flame up to medium. Using tongs, grasp one sheet of nori at a time and slowly drag it over the flame to toast, taking care not to let it catch fire. Let it cool and break it into a few smaller pieces.

IN the bowl of a mini food processor or mini blender (such as NutriBullet) fitted with the blade attachment, combine the nori, chile flakes (if using), sesame seeds, and salt and pulse until ground. Remove and set aside.

TO MAKE ON THE STOVETOP

IN a wide, shallow pot, heat the avocado oil over high heat. Next comes a trick I learned from my friend Ree Drummond! Add 2 kernels of popcorn to the pan, cover, and wait until you hear them both pop. Once that happens, take the pan off the heat, scoop out the popped pieces, and add the rest of your popcorn. Swirl to coat in the oil, cover the pan again, and let it sit off the heat for 1 minute, then return the pan to medium-high heat and let it cook until the kernels start popping wildly, shaking the pan intermittently to avoid burning. When popping slows and almost stops, remove the pan from the heat and let sit covered another minute. Add the nori spice mix, cover, and shake to coat the popcorn. Place in a large bowl and serve.

TO MAKE IN AN AIR POPPER

PLACE the avocado oil in a spray bottle. Add the popcorn kernels to an air popper according to instructions and pop into a large bowl. When popping is complete, lightly spray the popcorn with oil. Immediately toss with the nori seasoning and enjoy!

Lemon-Fennel Ginger Tea

Well, this isn't much in the way of a snack, but it is something I love to make—whether first thing in the morning to warm up my whole system or in the afternoon if I want something to stave off my craving for that second cup of coffee and boost my digestion at the same time.

—————————————— **MAKES 2 SERVINGS** ——————————————

2 inches fresh ginger, chopped

1 tablespoon plus 2 teaspoons fennel seeds, crushed

4 cups filtered water

Juice from 1 lemon (about 2 tablespoons)

2 teaspoons Date Syrup (page 244, optional)

HEAT the ginger, fennel seed, and water in a small saucepan over medium heat until simmering. Simmer for 5 minutes, then remove from the heat and steep for 5 minutes. Strain and discard the ginger pieces and fennel seeds.

STIR in the lemon juice and Date Syrup (if using).

The Most Addictive Kale Chips

These are my kids' favorite snack. Just so we're clear, they love cheese crackers and barbecue chips and all those yummy things, too, but they still prefer these vegetables baked in the oven with nutritional yeast. They're that good. I suggest you make some immediately.

MAKES 4 SERVINGS

1 bunch curly kale, stemmed and leaves torn into bite-size pieces

2 tablespoons extra-virgin olive oil

½ teaspoon garlic salt

2 tablespoons nutritional yeast

PREHEAT the oven to 350ºF.

BE sure the kale is very dry after washing. Massage the olive oil into the kale and divide between two sheet pans. Sprinkle with the garlic salt and nutritional yeast.

BAKE for 8 to 12 minutes, rotating the pans halfway through top to bottom and front to back, until the kale is golden and crispy. Let the chips cool before serving (this helps with extra crisping).

WE never have leftovers, but if you do, you can store them in an airtight container on the counter for up to 3 days.

Easy Seeded Cracker Bark

These crackers are great to have around whether you want to create a quick open-faced sandwich, use them to scoop dip, or crush and crumble a few over your favorite salad for extra salty crunch. The cumin seeds really amp up the flavor, and the flax, chia, and sunflower seeds offer tons of protein and fiber to keep you nice and full.

½ cup pepitas

½ cup raw sunflower seeds

¼ cup whole flaxseeds

⅔ cup ground flaxseed

2 tablespoons chia seeds

¼ cup sesame seeds

2 teaspoons cumin seeds

2 tablespoons coconut oil, melted

1 teaspoon sea salt

1 teaspoon flaky sea salt

PREHEAT the oven to 325°F.

IN a medium bowl, combine the pepitas, sunflower seeds, whole flaxseeds, ground flaxseed, chia seeds, sesame seeds, cumin seeds, coconut oil, sea salt, and ½ cup warm water. Stir and let sit for 5 minutes. A stiffer dough will form as the water is absorbed.

DIVIDE the dough in half. Roll out each half between two sheets of parchment paper to ¼ inch thick. Transfer each rolled dough on the parchment to a separate sheet pan. Sprinkle with the flaky sea salt and bake for 40 to 45 minutes, rotating the pans top to bottom and front to back halfway through, until the crackers are golden brown and fragrant. Let cool completely so they get nice and crispy, then break into pieces.

STORE in an airtight container for up to 1 week.

Italian Roasted Chickpeas

These roasted chickpeas pack protein, fiber, and a little bit of healthy fat to fill you up and keep you going—and satisfy that salty snack craving. They could not be easier to make, and the way roasting crisps the chickpea skins as the moisture evaporates from within the bean creates an extra-decadent crunch-within-a-crunch experience you're really going to like. Feel free to add pretty much any flavoring you want—I've done curry and Mexican spices like cumin and chipotle, but I always come back to this easy Italian herb version with rosemary, thyme, chile flakes—just leave that last bandmate out if you don't like it spicy.

———————————————— **MAKES 4 SERVINGS** ————————————————

Two 15-ounce cans chickpeas, drained and rinsed

3 tablespoons extra-virgin olive oil

2 teaspoons dried rosemary leaves

2 teaspoons fresh thyme or 1 teaspoon dried thyme

¼ teaspoon crushed red chile flakes (optional)

¾ teaspoon sea salt

2 tablespoons grated Pecorino Romano cheese (optional)

2 tablespoons chopped fresh parsley (optional)

PREHEAT the oven to 400°F.

PLACE the chickpeas in a dish towel and pat until very dry. You can discard any skins that fall away.

TOSS the chickpeas, olive oil, rosemary, thyme, chile flakes (if using), and salt in large bowl. Spread evenly on a sheet pan.

ROAST for 30 to 40 minutes, flipping halfway through, until crispy.

REMOVE and let cool for a couple of minutes. Toss with the Pecorino Romano (if using) and parsley (if using) and serve, or store in an airtight container on the counter for up to 3 days.

Smoked Eggplant Dip

I consider smoked eggplant dip to be hummus's lesser known, potentially more interesting (!!!) cousin. Now, I love hummus—I have three recipes for it coming up next! It is rich and full of protein, and has enjoyed the greatest PR ever bestowed upon a humble bean dip. But there is something about generously roasting and charring eggplant, scooping out the creamy flesh, and mashing it together with tahini and lemon and garlic and spices and herbs until it is smooth and sumptuous that just feels . . . special. This particular preparation is exactly the way I love my food to be: simple but elevated, extremely flavorful from a few choice ingredients, healthy without ever letting you know it, and as delicious fresh as it is the next day. Dip just about anything into it and enjoy!

MAKES 4 SERVINGS
---

1 medium globe eggplant (about 1½ pounds), pierced all over with a fork or paring knife

2 tablespoons extra-virgin olive oil, plus more for garnish

½ teaspoon cumin seeds

⅓ cup tahini

Juice from 1 lemon (about 2 tablespoons)

1 garlic clove, minced

Pinch of cayenne pepper

½ teaspoon sweet paprika, plus more for garnish

Sea salt, to taste

2 tablespoons chopped fresh parsley

2 tablespoons chopped fresh mint

Carrot sticks and celery sticks, to serve

Easy Seeded Cracker Bark (page 231), to serve

PREHEAT the broiler or grill to medium-high heat.

IF using the broiler, place the eggplant on a sheet pan about 3 inches under the heat. Char for 20 to 30 minutes under the broiler or 15 to 20 minutes on the grill, rotating carefully with tongs every few minutes to char on all sides. This can also be done on top of a gas burner turned to medium heat. Place the eggplant directly on the gas burner and char for 15 to 20 minutes, rotating every few minutes to char on all sides.

TRANSFER the eggplant to a bowl, cover with plastic wrap, and let cool completely.

MEANWHILE, heat the olive oil and cumin seeds in a small sauté pan over medium heat until toasted and fragrant, 1 to 2 minutes. Remove from the heat and let cool.

CUT the eggplant in half, scoop out the flesh, and place it in a medium bowl. Discard the skins. Use two forks to mash the flesh until mostly smooth but still textured. Add the cumin seeds and olive oil, tahini, lemon juice, garlic, cayenne, and paprika and mix until smooth and creamy. Season with salt to taste. (To assemble in a food processor: Combine the roasted eggplant flesh and additional ingredients in a food processor fitted with the blade attachment, then puree until creamy and smooth.)

PLACE the dip in a serving bowl and garnish with an additional drizzle of olive oil and sprinkle of paprika, then scatter with the parsley and mint. Serve with the carrots and celery and Easy Seeded Cracker Bark.

Classic Hummus

Hummus is enjoying a tidal wave of popularity these days for its excellent ability to make anything you care to spread or dollop it onto taste a whole lot better. I've always loved it as an amazingly flavorful protein boost to sandwiches and salads, and as an easy dip, but I especially love that my kids *love* it—and it's therefore always on hand in my kitchen.

Once you taste how much fresher, fluffier, and richer it is when you make it from scratch, you'll have a hard time going back to store-bought. This recipe uses canned beans because it's ready in under five minutes. But the more traditional (and more delicious) version would be to start with dried chickpeas, soak them overnight, cook them just to tender, and then continue as described. (See Cooking Dried Chickpeas, page 239, for details.) Fresh hummus, made from chickpeas still warm from cooking, is simply life changing!

———————— **MAKES 4 SERVINGS** ————————

One 15-ounce can chickpeas, drained and liquid reserved

½ cup tahini

2 tablespoons extra-virgin olive oil, plus more for garnish

2 garlic cloves

¼ teaspoon ground cumin

Juice from 1 lemon (about 2 tablespoons)

Sea salt, to taste

2 teaspoons Crunchy Dukkah (page 256), to garnish

IN the bowl of a food processor fitted with the blade attachment, combine the chickpeas, tahini, olive oil, garlic, cumin, and lemon juice and blend until smooth. Add 4 to 5 tablespoons of the reserved chickpea liquid, season with salt, and blend until creamy. Transfer to a bowl and garnish with a drizzle of olive oil and the Crunchy Dukkah.

NOTE. If you want super-smooth hummus, peel the skins off the chickpeas and discard before blending!

Beet Hummus

Add some beets, they make it pink! And boost your folate and iron, if you're into that sort of thing.

1 medium beet, peeled

3 tablespoons extra-virgin olive oil, plus more for garnish

¾ cup canned chickpeas, drained and liquid reserved

½ cup tahini

2 garlic cloves

¼ teaspoon ground cumin

¼ teaspoon ground coriander

Juice from 1 lemon (about 2 tablespoons)

Sea salt, to taste

2 teaspoons Crunchy Dukkah (page 256), to garnish

PREHEAT the oven to 400°F.

PLACE the beet on a piece of foil and drizzle with 1 tablespoon of the olive oil. Wrap tightly and roast for 30 minutes, until tender. Let cool completely. Roughly chop.

IN the bowl of a food processor fitted with the blade attachment, combine the beet, remaining 2 tablespoons olive oil, chickpeas, tahini, garlic, cumin, coriander, and lemon juice and season with salt. Blend until smooth and creamy. Add any reserved chickpea liquid, if needed, and continue to blend until smooth. Garnish with a drizzle of olive oil and the Crunchy Dukkah.

Green Hummus

Hummus of another color! This one is lean, green, and fantastically full of minerals and antioxidants.

───────────── MAKES 4 SERVINGS ─────────────

2 cups packed baby spinach

¼ cup chopped fresh chives (cut into 1-inch sections)

¼ cup fresh cilantro leaves

One 15-ounce can chickpeas, drained and liquid reserved

½ cup tahini

2 tablespoons extra-virgin olive oil, plus more for garnish

2 garlic cloves

½ teaspoon sweet paprika, plus more for garnish

¼ teaspoon ground cumin

Juice from 1 lemon (about 2 tablespoons)

½ teaspoon sea salt

2 teaspoons Crunchy Dukkah (page 256), to garnish

IN the bowl of a food processor fitted with the blade attachment, combine the spinach, chives, cilantro, chickpeas, tahini, olive oil, garlic, paprika, cumin, lemon juice, and salt. Blend until smooth, add 2 to 4 tablespoons of the reserved chickpea liquid, and continue blending until creamy. Transfer to a serving bowl and garnish with a drizzle of olive oil, a sprinkle of paprika, and the Crunchy Dukkah.

COOKING DRIED CHICKPEAS

If you want the creamiest, fluffiest, most mind-blowing hummus, you must start with dried chickpeas. Here's how to cook them to tender perfection, which you can then whip into the lightest protein-packed bean dip around. PS. If you have a pressure cooker, you can speed the cook time up considerably!

Measure ¾ cup dried chickpeas. Look through them and discard any stones. Place the chickpeas in a large bowl and cover with several inches of cool water. Soak at room temperature overnight, about 12 hours. (If you don't have time to soak overnight, use the quick-soak method. Place the chickpeas in a large pot and cover with several inches of water. Bring to a boil over high heat and boil for 1 minute. Then cover the pot and remove from the heat. Let the chickpeas soak for 1 hour, then drain and rinse again.)

Drain and rinse the chickpeas. Place in a large pot with a pinch of salt and cover with several inches of water. Bring to a boil, then reduce to a simmer and cook, partially covered, for 1½ to 2 hours, until just tender (add more water if necessary). Drain, reserving some of the cooking liquid, and run under cold water.

flavor boosters

WHEN IT COMES TO CREATING FAST MEALS FULL OF FLAVOR,

bright boosters, multitasking marinades, and homemade pantry staples will become your best friends. There is nothing Quick-Pickled Onions can't juice-ify, a dash of Date Syrup can't sweet-ify, a drizzle of Chili Sesame Oil can't gloss-ify, a sprinkling of Crunchy Dukkah can't crunch-ify . . . Make room on your shelves for the backup dancers that will save you time, elevate your cooking, and just maybe steal the show.

DATE SYRUP 244

EASY TOMATILLO SALSA (SALSA VERDE) 245

QUICK-PICKLED ONIONS 246

PICO DE GALLO 249

VEGAN CHIPOTLE AIOLI 250

SWEET AND SPICY MUSTARD 251

CHILI SESAME OIL 253

EVERYDAY SUNFLOWER SEED CHEESELESS PESTO 254

PARSLEY AND MINT GREMOLATA 255

CRUNCHY DUKKAH 256

HERBED YOGURT DIP 257

CILANTRO-PEANUT CHUTNEY 258

CAPER AIOLI 259

LIME MISO SAUCE 260

BARBECUE SAUCE 261

Chocolate–Almond Butter Banana Coins

I started making these when I realized you could slice ripe bananas really thin, freeze them, then puree them in your blender into something that tastes exactly like ice cream. I used to make it all the time—and it was excellent. Then I realized that adding almond butter to that mix made it even thicker and creamier. So I started spreading almond butter in between two of the thin banana coins and freezing them like sandwich cookies for even easier blending. Well, one day . . . one such stack fell in my mouth before it could be pureed. And the rest is history.

These are so insanely easy—and highly satisfying if you're into cold, creamy, sweet treats. I make them with my kids all the time, and they're big fans of the Jackson Pollock–inspired approach of just splattering (ahem, drizzling) melted chocolate and warm almond butter over top of the thin banana coins in a wild zigzag of flavor before freezing. And since it keeps them occupied for a solid 10 minutes and is even easier than my original sandwich method, this is the process I'm sharing with you here. But do what sounds most delicious to you! You can also make the sandwiches and *then* drizzle them with chocolate and a sprinkle of sea salt before freezing. I think that sounds pretty fabulous right about now. Excuse me.

Pro tip: Pull them out of the freezer and let them thaw about a minute before biting in for an extra-luscious texture.

MAKES 1 TO 2 SERVINGS

1 ripe banana, peeled and cut into ½-inch rounds

1.5 ounces unsweetened chocolate, roughly chopped (¼ cup)

1 teaspoon Date Syrup (page 244)

2 tablespoons unsweetened natural almond butter

1 teaspoon coconut oil

Flaky sea salt, to garnish (optional)

LINE a sheet pan with parchment or wax paper. Place the banana rounds on the prepared sheet pan.

FILL a small saucepan with 1 inch of water and bring to a simmer over medium-low heat. Nestle a heatproof bowl in the saucepan but not touching the water. Add the chocolate and date syrup and stir until melted and smooth, about 5 minutes. Set aside.

PLACE a second heatproof bowl over the simmering water and add the almond butter and coconut oil and stir until smooth and runny, another 5 minutes.

DRIZZLE the dark chocolate and almond butter over the banana coins. Sprinkle with the flaky sea salt (if using).

TRANSFER to the freezer until the coins are frozen and the chocolate and almond butter have set, at least 1 hour. Store the coins in an airtight container or zip-top bag in the freezer for up to 2 weeks.

Peach and Papaya "Sorbet"

I crave this anytime the weather turns warm. It is richly thick, sun-sweetened with peaches and papaya, and gets so nice and creamy from the coconut milk. This recipe can easily be adapted to most fruit combinations you love. Just make sure you have at least half your fruit coming from very creamy choices, like papaya, mango, or banana, to ensure your mix doesn't get too icy—though even icy is refreshing.

MAKES 4 SERVINGS

1 cup frozen peaches

1 cup frozen papaya or mango cubes

½ cup light coconut milk, well shaken

1 vanilla bean, scraped (optional)

½ teaspoon pure vanilla extract

2 tablespoons Date Syrup (page 244)

1 cup ice

COMBINE the peaches, papaya cubes, coconut milk, vanilla bean seeds (if using), vanilla, Date Syrup, ice, and ½ cup water in a high-speed blender. Blend until smooth but slightly icy.

SERVE immediately or store in an airtight container in the freezer. If storing in the freezer for an extended period of time, thaw at room temperature for 15 to 20 minutes, until scoopable.

Watermelon-Lime Ice Pops

My kids eat ice pops almost every day—Florida life! I was really underwhelmed by the options at my supermarket, all of which had so much sugar or random other ingredients I didn't understand the need for. Most juices (and many smoothies, too) can be turned into ice pops just by pouring them into a mold and freezing, so it struck me as silly to miss a chance to just experiment with our own blends. This has been one of our all-time favorites for its gorgeous hot-pink color, natural sweetness, and the bit of lime that makes it taste a little like exotic limeade.

And while eating them cold from the freezer is a win for everyone, I have to tell you a sad story. Sometimes I find one abandoned on the counter that has started to melt and I'm forced to blend it into a fast, frozen watermelon margarita with a couple of extra ice cubes and a splash of tequila. That is really the worst.

───────────────── **MAKES 5 SERVINGS** ─────────────────

1 pound seedless watermelon, cut into 1-inch cubes (about 2 cups)

2 tablespoons Date Syrup (page 244)

Juice from 2 limes (about ¼ cup)

COMBINE the watermelon, Date Syrup, and lime juice in a high-speed blender. Blend until smooth. If the mixture is not blending well, add a splash of water or more lime juice and process until very smooth. Pour the watermelon mixture into ice-pop molds fitted with a stick and freeze for at least 4 hours, preferably overnight, until set.

NOTE. If you want your ice pops to be a bit more filling and creamy, try adding a bit of goat or sheep milk yogurt to the blender with your juice for a tangy protein boost!

Blackberry and Plum Crumble

Is there anything better than a warm berry crumble, bubbling with thick, garnet juices and scattered with a sweet, crunchy, nutty topping? I think not. This is just like all the ones you've had before, only without all that pesky refined sugar and flour and stuff.

--- MAKES 6 SERVINGS ---

OAT TOPPING

¾ cup almond flour

1 cup gluten-free rolled oats

½ teaspoon ground cinnamon

¼ teaspoon ground cardamom

½ teaspoon sea salt

1 tablespoon Date Syrup (page 244)

3 tablespoons coconut oil, melted

½ teaspoon pure vanilla extract

¼ cup full-fat goat or sheep milk yogurt, to serve (optional)

BLACKBERRY AND PLUM FILLING

5 cups fresh blackberries

2 fresh ripe plums, pitted and sliced

1 inch fresh ginger, peeled and grated (optional)

Zest and juice from 1 lemon (about 1 teaspoon zest and 2 tablespoons juice)

2 tablespoons Date Syrup (page 244)

1 tablespoon tapioca flour

PREHEAT the oven to 350°F.

TO make the oat topping, combine the almond flour, oats, cinnamon, cardamom, sea salt, Date Syrup, coconut oil, and vanilla in a medium bowl until crumbly. Refrigerate for 10 minutes.

MEANWHILE, make the blackberry filling. In a large bowl, mix the blackberries, plums, ginger (if using), lemon zest and juice, Date Syrup, and tapioca flour until combined. Place the filling into an 8 x 8-inch baking dish.

SPRINKLE the topping over the blackberry mixture. Cover with foil and bake for 25 minutes. Uncover and bake for another 15 minutes, until the crumble is golden and the filling is bubbling. Let cool for 10 minutes and serve with a dollop of sheep or goat milk yogurt (if using).

Oatmeal Cookie Balls

Oh, have I got a treat for you!!! Oatmeal cookie balls you can eat for breakfast! I'm sensing a theme in this chapter. Insane, you say! Truly, except that they get their nutty richness and sweet warmth from oatmeal, nuts, spices, flaxseeds, Date Syrup, and a few raisins. and that, my friends, means they are every bit as breakfast-as-usual as a granola bar. Only shaped like a cookie ball. In the dessert section.

— **MAKES 12 OR 13 BALLS** —

1 cup gluten-free rolled oats

1 cup walnuts or pecans

¼ cup whole flaxseeds

½ cup unsweetened natural almond butter

1 teaspoon ground cinnamon

¼ teaspoon ground nutmeg

1 teaspoon pure vanilla extract

3 tablespoons Date Syrup (page 244)

½ teaspoon sea salt

¼ cup raisins

IN the bowl of a food processor fitted with the blade attachment, combine ½ cup of the oats, the walnuts, and the flaxseeds and pulse until finely ground. Add the almond butter, cinnamon, nutmeg, vanilla, Date Syrup, and salt and pulse until a smooth dough forms that's about the consistency of cookie dough. If the dough is too thick, add 2 to 4 tablespoons of hot water to loosen it. Transfer to a large bowl and stir in the remaining ½ cup oats and the raisins. Refrigerate for 10 minutes.

SCOOP the dough into 1-inch balls (2 tablespoons each) and roll until smooth. Store in an airtight container in the refrigerator for 1 week or the freezer for 1 month.

Coconut Chocolate Seed Clusters

Oh, you like coconut? Wait, and you like crunchy salty things in chocolate? Hang on, hang on. Do you *also* like a teensy-eensy bit of chew, just the slightest caramelly experience binding all the crunchy salty things together??? Ohhhhh, okay. Well, then you're really going to love these.

MAKES 34 CLUSTERS

2 cups unsweetened coconut flakes

1 cup roasted salted pepitas

1 cup roasted salted sunflower seeds

3 tablespoons Date Syrup (page 244)

2 tablespoons tapioca flour

4 ounces unsweetened chocolate, chopped (2/3 cup)

1 tablespoon coconut oil

2 teaspoons coconut sugar

PREHEAT the oven to 350°F. Line two sheet pans with parchment paper.

PLACE the coconut flakes, pepitas, sunflower seeds, Date Syrup, and tapioca flour in a large bowl and mix to combine. Scoop by the heaping tablespoon onto the prepared sheet pan. Lightly pinch each together to form a cluster.

BAKE for 5 to 7 minutes, until the coconut is golden brown. Remove and let cool completely.

FILL a small saucepan with 1 inch of water and bring to a simmer over medium-low heat. Nestle a heatproof bowl in the saucepan but not touching the water. Add the chocolate and stir until melted and smooth, about 5 minutes. Stir in the coconut sugar until dissolved.

DRIZZLE each cluster with the melted chocolate in a happy little haphazard pattern.

CHILL the clusters in the freezer for 8 to 10 minutes, until the chocolate has set. Serve or store in an airtight container in the refrigerator for up to 1 week.

Sliced Mango and Citrus with Lime, Chile, and Smoked Sea Salt

Just a simple, easy as 1–2–3 palate cleanser that I have many times a week and always find refreshing and satisfying. If you've ever been to Mexico City, you may have seen fruit vendors there selling ripe, sweet, juicy fruit, sprinkled generously with Tajín—a lime-scented chile salt seasoning. And since I sadly have never been to Mexico City (it's on my bucket list!), this is my ode to what I can only imagine is a very happy, sun-drenched bite. If your fruit isn't very sweet, go ahead and drizzle the plate with a teaspoon or two of Date Syrup (page 244) to amp it up.

──────────────── **MAKES 4 SERVINGS** ────────────────

1 navel orange

1 ruby grapefruit

1 ripe mango, sliced into thin half-moons

Juice from 1 lime (about 2 tablespoons)

½ teaspoon chipotle chile powder or another smoky/sweet ground chile powder, to garnish

Pinch of smoked or flaky sea salt, to garnish

USING a paring knife, thinly cut the top and bottom off the orange and grapefruit so that the fruit sits flat. Working from top to bottom, carefully remove the rind of the orange and grapefruit, rotating as you cut downward. When the rind has all been removed, cut the orange and grapefruit into thin wheels.

ARRANGE the orange wheels, grapefruit wheels, and mango slices on a platter. Squeeze the lime juice on top and sprinkle with the chile powder and smoky salt. Enjoy.

Coconut Joy Cups

These are less in the "light" category and more in the "I want to treat myself to something I love using only wholesome ingredients" camp. I love the play of creamy almond butter and shredded coconut for texture with a hidden gem whole almond tucked into each, and rich, faintly bitter chocolate is the perfect foil to all that sweetness.

MAKES 12 CUPS

8 ounces unsweetened chocolate, chopped (1⅓ cups)

1 tablespoon coconut oil

2 tablespoons coconut sugar

¼ cup unsweetened shredded coconut

¼ cup creamy almond butter, warmed

1 teaspoon pure vanilla extract

¼ teaspoon sea salt

1 teaspoon Date Syrup (page 244)

12 raw almonds

Flaky sea salt, to garnish

LINE a mini muffin tin with 12 paper liners.

PLACE the chocolate, coconut oil, and coconut sugar in a heatproof bowl and set over a saucepan with 1 inch of simmering water, making sure the bowl is not touching the water. Stir until the chocolate is melted and the sugar has dissolved. (You can also use the microwave. Heat in 15-second intervals, stirring in between, until smooth.)

POUR a thin layer of chocolate (I like to use a liquid measuring cup!) into the bottom of each liner. Place in the freezer and let harden, about 10 minutes.

MEANWHILE, in a medium bowl, combine the shredded coconut, almond butter, vanilla, salt, and Date Syrup. When the chocolate has set, roll the coconut mixture into 12 balls and place in the center of each cup. Press an almond into the top of each coconut ball. Top each muffin cup with the remaining melted chocolate until filled. Sprinkle the tops with the flaky sea salt.

FREEZE for 10 minutes or until set. Enjoy immediately or store in an airtight container in the refrigerator for up to 1 week or the freezer for 1 to 2 months (from frozen, they are most delicious and creamy if you let them thaw for 5 to 10 minutes at room temperature before eating).

NOTE. If you want all coconut, all the time, try making these with coconut butter to replace the almond butter! A velvety spread made from ground fresh coconut, it is packed with nutrients, fat, and fiber—and ultra-pure, intense coconut flavor, which I love.

Banana Brûlée

This is just about the easiest thing you could possibly make with the most *insane* payoff. When I tell you we cannot stop eating these things, believe me—they're that good. You basically peel a banana and rub it lightly with a tiny bit of coconut oil, sprinkle with coconut sugar, and broil for a few minutes to create a creamy, sweet, slightly melty, crème brûlée-style pudding. It is beyond. If you have five minutes and a banana, go make it immediately.

MAKES 4 SERVINGS
---

4 firm ripe bananas, peeled

2 tablespoons coconut oil, melted

1 teaspoon pure vanilla extract

2 tablespoons coconut sugar

Sea salt, to garnish

ARRANGE the oven rack about 5 inches away from the broiler. Preheat the broiler. Slice the bananas in half lengthwise.

COMBINE the coconut oil and vanilla in a small bowl. Rub the coconut oil mixture all over the banana halves and place cut side up on a sheet pan. Broil until slightly softened, about 2 minutes.

SPRINKLE the bananas with the coconut sugar. Broil again until the sugar melts and creates a glossy surface, another 2 minutes (keep watch so the broiler doesn't burn the sugar!). Sprinkle with a pinch of sea salt before serving.

Dosa with Warm Dates, Yogurt, and Tahini

I saved this recipe for last for good reason. On the one hand, it's a bit complicated. It involves pureeing rice, lentils, and peas into a rich, frothy, fermenting batter. Then waiting overnight for your dosa batter to hydrate. Then cooking that batter into what are essentially thin, flexible, soft (but also crisp!) pancakes. These are not for any old impatient moment when you need a little something sweet.

You need kitchen confidence to attempt these, which I hope the pages of this book and your time in your kitchen, making happy little messes and big, delicious bites, will give you in spades! And once you master the technique, you'll find yourself whipping up casual dosas to layer with creamy tahini and warm dates as often as your heart desires. It is truly an "eat your heart out!" moment, when something that tastes so luxurious is truly clean, worthy of your attention and indulgence, and fills you with yummy abundance. It's something you did for yourself just because you could. Which feels damn good in my book. So you made it to the final recipe!! And you earned it. I hope you enjoy.

MAKES ABOUT 22 DOSAS, TO SERVE 4 TO 6

DOSAS

½ cup urad dal (skinned black whole lentils)

2 tablespoons chana dal (Bengal gam, known as split chickpeas), or yellow split peas

Pinch of fenugreek seeds

1½ cups short-grain white rice

1 teaspoon noniodized salt (important for fermentation—check the label!)

Coconut oil, for cooking

Full-fat goat or sheep milk yogurt, to serve

WARM DATES

1 tablespoon coconut oil

12 Medjool dates, pitted and cut into long strips

2 tablespoons orange juice (fresh is best but not essential)

Sea salt, to taste

1 teaspoon pure vanilla extract

TAHINI SAUCE

1 cup tahini

½ teaspoon sea salt, plus more to taste

TO make the dosas, combine the lentils and split chickpeas in a fine-mesh sieve and rinse under cold water until the water runs clear. Transfer to a large pot or bowl and add the fenugreek seeds. Cover with cool water and let soak at room temperature for about 6 hours and up to overnight. Repeat the same process with the rice in a separate bowl, excluding the fenugreek seeds.

DRAIN the lentil mixture and transfer to a high-speed blender. Add ½ teaspoon of the noniodized salt and ¾ cup water and blend until very smooth and frothy. The batter should be a thick, pouring consistency. Transfer to a large pot or bowl.

DRAIN the rice and transfer to the blender. Add the remaining ½ teaspoon noniodized salt and ⅔ cup water and blend until very smooth. The goal is to reach the same consistency as the lentil puree, so add more water by the tablespoon to thin as needed. When blending the rice, there may be a slight texture from the rice granules, but overall it should be very smooth.

ADD the pureed rice to the pureed lentil mixture and use your hand to stir well to combine (using your hand actually helps to begin the fermentation process—plus, it's fun!).

COVER with a plate and let ferment in a warm place for 10 to 12 hours, until the batter has risen and is fluffy with bubbles. Don't rush this; if it doesn't look bubbly, it may need to ferment longer. Cook immediately or store in the refrigerator for up to 3 days until ready to use (see Note on page 312).

MEANWHILE, to make the warm dates, heat the coconut oil in a medium saucepan over medium-low heat. Add the dates and cook, stirring, until they begin to sizzle and their skins become slightly translucent, 2 to 3 minutes. Add the orange juice, ½ cup water, and a pinch of sea salt. Simmer until the mixture resembles a thick, jammy, rustic compote, about 5 minutes. Stir in the vanilla and remove from the heat to cool slightly. Cover to keep warm until ready to serve.

WHEN ready to make the dosas, note that the batter may be fairly thick after fermentation. It should coat the back of a spoon, like a thin pancake batter (though not quite as thin as crepe batter), and make ribbons when drizzled in the bowl. If you're questioning proper thickness, place a small test amount of the batter in a separate bowl and thin with water by the tablespoon until the desired consistency is reached. Cook this batter as a test before adding more water to the remaining batter.

HEAT a griddle or medium cast-iron pan over medium heat. Add a small amount of coconut oil (start with ¼ teaspoon), just enough to thinly coat the griddle surface, rubbing gently and carefully with a paper towel to distribute. Ladle about ¼ cup of the dosa batter onto the griddle and spread in a circular motion with the back of the ladle to make a thin layer of batter. When the dosa begins to set, spoon a little bit of coconut oil around its edges to help browning and avoid sticking. When the first side is golden, about 3 minutes, flip and finish cooking on the other side, about 1 minute. Transfer to a plate. Sprinkle some water droplets on

(recipe continues)

the griddle and clean carefully with a paper towel before making the next dosa. If the pan becomes too hot and the batter isn't easy to spread, turn the heat down to medium-low and continue.

TO make the tahini sauce, whisk the tahini, ¾ cup ice water, and sea salt together in a medium bowl. The mixture will look broken and seized at first, but continue mixing until thick, combined, and smooth. Season with additional salt as desired.

TO serve the dosas, you can either fold the dosas in thirds around a central slather of yogurt and a spoonful of dates drizzled with tahini, or you can plate the sauces and dates and serve the dosas on the side to be torn into bite-size pieces that you then use to scoop up individual bites, perfectly personalized to balance the flavors just the way you like!

NOTE. Want to get a head start? Dosa batter can be stored in the refrigerator for up to 3 days. Just check the consistency and thin with water as needed before cooking.

Chocolate Medjool Date Cake

Encore! Encore! Okay, just kidding—you get one more recipe! Because how could I let you go without dense, moist date cake—now with chocolate! It's as easy as throwing a bunch of things into a food processor. There's no gluten to overwork, only almond flour, which keeps this cake wonderfully hydrated even as it bakes up to a tender crumb.

MAKES 8 TO 10 SERVINGS

1 tablespoon coconut oil, for greasing

1 cup Medjool dates, pitted and roughly chopped

2 tablespoons chia seeds

1 teaspoon pure vanilla extract

1/3 cup unsweetened cocoa powder

1 teaspoon baking soda

1/2 teaspoon sea salt

1 1/4 cups almond flour

1 large egg, lightly beaten

1/2 cup full-fat goat or sheep milk yogurt

2 tablespoons Date Syrup (page 244, optional), to serve

PREHEAT the oven to 350ºF. Grease an 8 x 8-inch baking dish with the coconut oil and line it with two overlapping pieces of parchment paper, letting the paper overhang on all four sides to act as handles for easy removal after baking.

PLACE the dates and 1/2 cup warm water in the bowl of a food processor fitted with the blade attachment. Pulse until incorporated, then blend until smooth, about 30 seconds. Add the chia seeds, vanilla, cocoa powder, baking soda, salt, almond flour, egg, and yogurt and pulse again until just combined and smooth, scraping down the sides of the bowl as needed. Pour the batter into the baking dish and smooth the top.

BAKE for 25 to 30 minutes, until an inserted toothpick comes out clean. Let cool for 10 minutes in the pan, then transfer to a wire rack to cool completely.

SLICE and serve with a drizzle of Date Syrup, if desired.

ACKNOWLEDGMENTS

There are no sufficient amounts of praise and thanks to spoon, lavish, and heap upon the incredible team of family, friends, confidantes, and crew who made this book possible. Back in 2019, when we first began the work of bringing it to life, the world looked quite different. Over the intervening years, we navigated a creative, collaborative project through lockdowns, surges, and upheaval to create something sturdy, lasting, and useful that you now hold in your hands. I feel so lucky and proud that together we made it real!

To start at the beginning, every bite I take is a lesson. And all those lessons begin in my mother's and grandmother's kitchens. I dedicated this book to my children, because I hope that the joy of creating, exploring, and savoring life through food just might be hereditary. It is one of my greatest daily pleasures, and I am endlessly grateful for the way in which my family has shown me what prioritizing and protecting your joy creates—everyday magic! And also because four pregnancies contributed a great deal to my own personal need for this book to exist, and I am so grateful to my babies for the continued delicious inspiration in all that I do!

One hundred and fifty recipes is a lot. Laura Arnold, you are an actual earth angel. I don't think any other human could have met all my musings and midnight emails, always with such culinary wisdom and a beaming smile to boot.

This epic food team continues with its other essential half: Frances Boswell, who calls herself a food stylist but I would argue is really a food conjurer par excellence. Every plate becomes so much more than the sum of its humble parts in your hands, droplets of olive oil or honey or flecks of trimmed herbs and salt anointing mere mortal food with epic craveability. Your attending ladies of the kitchen, Leila Clifford and Laura Kinsey

Dolph, will know all about that! I am full with so many delicious memories of our kitchen escapades.

When it came to making these recipes leap from the page and hopefully approximate the closest thing we have to scratch-and-sniff cookbooks: Amy Neunsinger—cascading, filtering light whisperer with your magic eye and an endless ability to make me laugh just before I fall over in awe at the art you create. Johnny Miller—the breathtaking photos that sprang from your camera as you chased me and my crazy brood color these pages with the ease and fun you effortlessly inspire. And to your teams: Andrew Mitchell, Hector Prida, Devon Guio, and Luc Decker—thank you for keeping us lit, synced, and snapping!

Sarah Smart, thank you for sourcing all the food-inspired color, handmade elegance, smooth, round edges and glorious textures (bring on all the plaster!), and patinaed antiques and freshly gilded accessories to create every scene as though it sprang from my dreams! Ali Summers, thank you for holding down the fort so brilliantly when all was extra topsy-turvy.

Thank you to David Larabell and my brilliant CAA family for so many years of support and believing!

Thank you to Cassie Jones, endlessly patient editor who still thinks my headnotes are funny after all these years! Jill Zimmerman, who somehow managed to keep track of every note, draft, and new submission seamlessly—a true miracle! And to Liate Stehlik, Ben Steinberg, Anwesha Basu, Kayleigh George, Shelby Peak, Renata De Oliveira, and Marta Durkin—what a great gift to be a part of this incredible William Morrow family. Thank you for all you do to bring your author's dreams to life.

To my dear friends and teammates who supported me throughout and most especially helped choose a title that adequately conveyed how much I wanted everyone who reads this book to understand the freedom and deliciousness taking good care of yourself should always represent.

And most of all—John. Our marriage is my most treasured wellspring of profound joy. Thank you for wearing all your hats, but especially for being mine. I love you.

UNIVERSAL CONVERSION CHART

OVEN TEMPERATURE EQUIVALENTS

250°F = 120°C

275°F = 135°C

300°F = 150°C

325°F = 160°C

350°F = 180°C

375°F = 190°C

400°F = 200°C

425°F = 220°C

450°F = 230°C

475°F = 240°C

500°F = 260°C

MEASUREMENT EQUIVALENTS

Measurements should always be level unless directed otherwise.

⅛ teaspoon = 0.5 mL

¼ teaspoon = 1 mL

½ teaspoon = 2 mL

1 teaspoon = 5 mL

1 tablespoon = 3 teaspoons = ½ fluid ounce = 15 mL

2 tablespoons = ⅛ cup = 1 fluid ounce = 30 mL

4 tablespoons = ¼ cup = 2 fluid ounces = 60 mL

5⅓ tablespoons = ⅓ cup = 3 fluid ounces = 80 mL

8 tablespoons = ½ cup = 4 fluid ounces = 120 mL

10⅔ tablespoons = ⅔ cup = 5 fluid ounces = 160 mL

12 tablespoons = ¾ cup = 6 fluid ounces = 180 mL

16 tablespoons = 1 cup = 8 fluid ounces = 240 mL

INDEX

Note: Page references in *italics* indicate photographs.

A

Aioli
    Caper, 259
    Vegan Chipotle, 250
Almond Butter
    –Chocolate Banana Coins, 293
    Coconut Joy Cups, 305
    Oatmeal Cookie Balls, 300, *301*
Almond(s)
    Coconut Joy Cups, 305
    Creamy Parsnip Soup with Manchego Crisps, 116–17, *119*
    Crispy Chicken Strips with Sweet and Spicy Mustard, 163
    Cucumber Melon Gazpacho, *130*, 131
    Dark Chocolate Energy Truffles, *288*, 289
    Gingersnap Granola Bars, *20*, 21
    and Oat Piecrust, 40–41
    Savory Granola with Thyme and Chile, *30*, 31
Anchovy Lemon Dressing, 281
Apple(s)
    Celery, and Cucumber, Clean Up Your Act Smoothie with, 54, *55*
    Creamy Parsnip Soup with Manchego Crisps, 116–17, *119*
    and Manchego, Watercress with, *72*, 73
    Poblano Chopped Chicken Salad with Creamy Cilantro-Lime Dressing, 83
Arugula
    Hummus and Roasted Veggie Morning Bowl, 36
    6-Minute Egg over Greens with Lemon-Anchovy Dressing, *34*, 35
    Summer Market Corn, Cucumber, and Crab Salad, *76*, 77
Asparagus, Leek, and Herb Quiche, *42*, 43
Avocados
    Barbecue Mushroom Tacos with Tomatillo Salsa, 108
    Chipotle Chicken Meatball Burrito Bowl, 152–53
    Scandi-Style Salmon Toast, 37, *39*
    Spinach and Crispy Tofu with Curried Tahini Dressing, 80, *81*
    Summer Market Corn, Cucumber, and Crab Salad, *76*, 77

B

Banana(s)
    Blue Seas Smoothie with Blueberry and Spirulina, 53
    Brûlée, 306, *307*
    Chai Turmeric Smoothie, 56, *57*
    Coins, Chocolate–Almond Butter, 293
    Eggs, and Yogurt, Magic Pancakes with, *16*, 17
    Pumpkin Muffins, *32*, 33
Barbecue Chicken Skewers, 189
Barbecue Mushroom Tacos with Tomatillo Salsa, 108
Barbecue Pulled Chicken on Crispy Smashed Japanese Yams, *164*, 165–66
Barbecue Sauce, 261
Bars, Gingersnap Granola, *20*, 21

Basil
    Easy Sunflower Seed Cheeseless Pesto, 254
    Green Goddess Dressing, *271*, 273
    Snow Peas, and Okra, Delivery Chicken with, *170*, 171
BBQ Chicken, Mama's, 140, *141*
Bean(s). *See also* Chickpea(s)
    Black, Lentil Burger with Vegan Chipotle Aioli, 104–5
    Chipotle Chicken Meatball Burrito Bowl, 152–53
    Endive and Tuna with Castelvetrano Olives, 90, *91*
    Feel-Good Turkey Meatloaf, 144–46, *145*
    Green, and Teriyaki Chicken, Sheet-Pan, 136
    Lightened-Up English Breakfast, *28*, 29
    Power Greens Soup with Charred Scallions, 127
    Spicy Slow-Cooker Chicken Chili with Black-Eyed Peas, 180–81
    White, and Cilantro-Peanut Chutney, Lamb Chops with, *176*, 177
Bee Pollen and Cantaloupe, Melonballer Smoothie with, 52
Beet(s)
    and Greens, Braised, with Walnuts, 190, *191*
    Hidden Veggie Waffles, 25
    Hummus, *237*, 238
    Quick Vegetarian Borscht with Lemon Horseradish Cream, 128, *129*
    and Watermelon, Pink Juice with, 60, *61*
Berry(ies)
    Baked Pears with Yogurt and Oats, *44*, 45
    Blackberry and Plum Crumble, 298, *299*
    Blueberry Oatmeal Bake, 22, *23*
    Blue Seas Smoothie with Blueberry and Spirulina, 53
    Raspberry Dark Chocolate Drops, 286, *287*
    Red, Slab Pie, 290–92, *291*
Bison Meatballs in Tomato Sauce, Sicilian-ish, 150–51
Blackberry and Plum Crumble, 298, *299*
Black-Eyed Peas, Spicy Slow-Cooker Chicken Chili with, 180–81
Blueberry
    Oatmeal Bake, 22, *23*
    and Spirulina, Blue Seas Smoothie with, 53
Bok Choy, Roasted, Sheet-Pan Miso-Glazed Sea Bass with, *142*, 143
Borscht, Quick Vegetarian, with Lemon Horseradish Cream, 128, *129*
Branzino Stuffed with Red Onion, Lemon, and Oregano, *178*, 179
Bread
    gluten-free seeded, DIY, 37
    Scandi-Style Salmon Toast, 37, *39*
Broccoli
    and Feta Scramble, Spicy, 24
    Power Greens Soup with Charred Scallions, 127
    Sheet-Pan Tandoori Chicken with, *158*, 159
Broccoli rabe
    Roasted, and Millet with Cherries, *192*, 193
Brussels Sprouts, Candied, Crispy Tofu with, 156, *157*

Burgers
  Cajun Salmon, 114, *115*
  Lentil Black Bean, with Vegan Chipotle Aioli, 104–5
Burrito Bowl, Chipotle Chicken Meatball, 152–53

C

Cabbage
  Asian Chopped Chicken Salad with Sweet Chili Soy
    Dressing, 86, 87
  Barbecue Mushroom Tacos with Tomatillo Salsa, 108
  Dumplings, Chicken and Scallion, 154–55
  Easy Veggie Pho with Coconut Broth, *124*, 125–26
  Quick Vegetarian Borcht with Lemon Horseradish Cream,
    128, *129*
  Rainbow Collard Wraps with Crispy Tofu, 100–101, *102–3*
  Slaw, Crunchy, Cilantro-Lime Halibut Tacos with, 109
  Spicy Crunchy Cauliflower Tacos with Ranch Slaw, *106*, 107
Cake, Chocolate Medjool Date, 313
Caper Aioli, 259
Carrot(s)
  -Ginger Dressing, 266, *269*
  -Ginger Shrimp Bowl, 175
  Hummus and Roasted Veggie Morning Bowl, 36
  Quick Vegetarian Borscht with Lemon Horseradish Cream,
    128, *129*
  Rainbow Collard Wraps with Crispy Tofu, 100–101, *102–3*
  and Red Lentil Soup, Lemony, 122, *123*
  Shrimp Summer Roll Lettuce Cups, 110, *111*
  Spinach and Crispy Tofu with Curried Tahini Dressing, 80,
    81
  and Turnips, Za'atar-Roasted, with Gremolata, 194, *195*
Cashews
  Asian Chopped Chicken Salad with Sweet Chili Soy
    Dressing, 86, 87
  Creamy Cilantro-Lime Dressing, 270, *271*
  Crunchy Dukkah, 256
  Vegan Spaghetti Squash Carbonara with Mushroom Bacon,
    168–69, *169*
Cauliflower
  Chickpea Coconut Curry, 137
  Melonballer Smoothie with Cantaloupe and Bee Pollen, 52
  Rice with Caramelized Onion and Hazelnuts, 198
  Roasted, with Scallions, Hazelnuts, and Dates, 214, *215*
  Spicy Crunchy, Tacos with Ranch Slaw, *106*, 107
  Tabbouleh, 82
Celery
  Apple, and Cucumber, Clean Up Your Act Smoothie with,
    54, 55
  Faux Chickpea "Tuna" Salad, *78*, 79
  Pickled Grapes, and Scallions, Lentils with, *70*, 71
  Summer Market Corn, Cucumber, and Crab Salad, *76*, 77
Celery Root and Figs, Spatchcock Chicken with, 172–74, *173*
Chai Turmeric Smoothie, 56, 57
Cheese
  Creamy Parsnip Soup with Manchego Crisps, 116–17, *119*
  Egg and Chutney Crepes, 96, *97*
  Red Berry Slab Pie, 290–92, *291*
  Roasted Butternut Squash Pasta Bake, 162
  Spicy Broccoli and Feta Scramble, 24
  Watercress with Apples and Manchego, 72, *73*
Cherries, Roasted Broccoli Rabe and Millet with, *192*, 193

Chia Seed(s)
  Affogato Oatmeal with Coffee and Coconut Cream, 27
  Easy Seeded Cracker Bark, 231, *234*
  Pudding, Strawberries and Cream, 46, *47*
Chicken
  Barbecue Pulled, on Crispy Smashed Japanese Yams, *164*,
    165–66
  BBQ, Mama's, 140, *141*
  Chili, Spicy Slow-Cooker, with Black-Eyed Peas, 180–81
  Chipotle, Meatball Burrito Bowl, 152–53
  Delivery, with Basil, Snow Peas, and Okra, *170*, 171
  how to spatchcock, 174
  Lightened-Up English Breakfast, 28, 29
  Meaty Greens Fried Rice, 204
  Paillard, Grilled, with Greek Salad, 84
  Poblano Chopped, Salad with Creamy Cilantro-Lime
    Dressing, 83
  Salad, Asian Chopped, with Sweet Chili Soy Dressing, 86,
    87
  and Scallion Cabbage Dumplings, 154–55
  Skewers, Barbecue, 189
  Skewers, Mediterranean, 186, *187*
  Skewers, Peanut-Chili, 188
  Soup with Lentils, 121
  Spatchcock, with Figs and Celery Root, 172–74, *173*
  Strips, Crispy, with Sweet and Spicy Mustard, 163
  Tandoori, with Broccoli, Sheet-Pan, *158*, 159
  Teriyaki, and Green Beans, Sheet-Pan, 136
  Thighs, Braised, with Fennel, Lemon, and Dates, 160, *161*
Chickpea Flour Crepe Wraps, 96, 98
Chickpea(s)
  Beet Hummus, 237, *238*
  Cauliflower Coconut Curry, 137
  Classic Hummus, 236, *237*
  Crispy Roasted Butternut Squash and Quinoa with Currant
    Vinaigrette, 210, *211*
  dried, cooking, 239
  Green Hummus, 237, 239
  Italian Roasted, 232, *233*
  "Tuna" Salad, Faux, *78*, 79
Chili, Spicy Slow-Cooker Chicken, with Black-Eyed Peas, 180–81
Chili-Garlic Japanese Yam Cubes, 220, *221*
Chili Sesame Oil, 252, *253*
Chili Soy Dressing, Sweet, 275
Chipotle Aioli, Vegan, 250
Chipotle and Cumin, Sweet and Spicy Pecans with, *222*, 223
Chipotle Chicken Meatball Burrito Bowl, 152–53
Chocolate
  –Almond Butter Banana Coins, 293
  Coconut Joy Cups, 305
  Coconut Seed Clusters, 302, *303*
  Dark, Energy Truffles, 288, 289
  Dark, Raspberry Drops, 286, *287*
  Medjool Date Cake, 313
Chutney, Cilantro-Peanut, 258, *271*
Cilantro
  -Lime Dressing, Creamy, 270, *271*
  -Lime Halibut Tacos with Crunchy Cabbage Slaw,
    109
  -Peanut Chutney, 258, *271*
Cinnamon, Rosemary, and Thyme Nut Mix, 224

Citrus. *See also* Lemon; Lime
    and Mango, Sliced, with Lime, Chile, and Smoked Sea Salt,
        304
    Vinaigrette, *277, 278*
Coconut
    Broth, Easy Veggie Pho with, *124,* 125–26
    Chickpea Cauliflower Curry, 137
    Chocolate Seed Clusters, *302, 303*
    Cream and Coffee, Affogato Oatmeal with, 27
    Forbidden Rice, 203
    Joy Cups, 305
Coffee and Coconut Cream, Affogato Oatmeal with, 27
Collard Green Sandwich Wraps, 99
Collard Wraps, Rainbow, with Crispy Tofu, *100–101, 102–3*
Cookie Balls, Oatmeal, *300, 301*
Corn, Cucumber, and Crab Salad, Summer Market, *76, 77*
Crab, Cucumber, and Corn Salad, Summer Market, *76, 77*
Cracker Bark, Easy Seeded, 231, *234*
Crepes, Egg and Chutney, *96, 97*
Crepe Wraps, Chickpea Flour, *96,* 98
Cucumber(s)
    Apple, and Celery, Clean Up Your Act Smoothie with, *54, 55*
    Carrot-Ginger Shrimp Bowl, 175
    Cauliflower Tabbouleh, 82
    Corn, and Crab Salad, Summer Market, *76, 77*
    Emerald Eyes Juice with Fresh Greens and Mint, 58
    Grilled Chicken Paillard with Greek Salad, 84
    Herbed Yogurt Dip, 257
    Melon Gazpacho, Creamy, *130, 131*
    Pink Juice with Watermelon and Beet, 60, *61*
    Rainbow Collard Wraps with Crispy Tofu, *100–101, 102–3*
    Scandi-Style Salmon Toast, 37, *39*
    Sesame-Soy Smashed, *208, 209*
Cumin
    and Chipotle, Sweet and Spicy Pecans with, *222, 223*
    Easy Seeded Cracker Bark, 231, *234*
Currant Vinaigrette, 279
Curried Tahini Dressing with Turmeric and Ginger, 266, 268
Curry, Chickpea Cauliflower Coconut, 137

D
Dairy-free milks
    Nut Milk, 62
    Oat Milk, 63
Date(s)
    Dark Chocolate Energy Truffles, *288, 289*
    Fennel, and Lemon, Braised Chicken Thighs with, 160, *161*
    Medjool, Chocolate Cake, 313
    Scallions, and Hazelnuts, Roasted Cauliflower with, 214, *215*
    Syrup, 244
    Warm, Yogurt, and Tahini, Dosa with, 308–12, *310–11*
Dips
    Beet Hummus, *237, 238*
    Classic Hummus, *236, 237*
    Green Hummus, *237, 239*
    Herbed Yogurt, 257
    Smoked Eggplant, *234, 235*
Dosa with Warm Dates, Yogurt, and Tahini, 308–12, *310–11*
Dressings
    Carrot-Ginger, 266, *269*
    Cilantro-Lime, Creamy, *270, 271*

Citrus Vinaigrette, *277, 278*
Currant Vinaigrette, 279
Curried Tahini, with Turmeric and Ginger, 266, 268
Greek, *276, 277*
Green Goddess, *271, 273*
Lemon Anchovy, 281
Peanut, Crunchy, 274
Ranch, Tangy, 280
Shallot Vinaigrette, 280
Sweet Chili Soy, 275
Tahini, Simple, *266, 267*
Drinks. *See also* Juices; Smoothies; Tea
Dukkah, Crunchy, 256
Dumplings, Chicken and Scallion Cabbage, 154–55

E
Eggplant
    Parm-less, with Simple Tomato Sauce, 205–6, *207*
    Smoked, Dip, *234, 235*
Egg(s)
    Bananas, and Yogurt, Magic Pancakes with, 16, *17*
    and Chutney Crepes, *96, 97*
    Kabocha Squash, and Quinoa Bowl, 18, *19*
    Lightened-Up English Breakfast, 28, *29*
    Meaty Greens Fried Rice, 204
    Salad, Middle Eastern, 68, *69*
    6-Minute, over Greens with Lemon-Anchovy Dressing, *34,*
        35
    Spicy Broccoli and Feta Scramble, 24
Endive
    Grilled Radicchio and Peach Salad, 88, *89*
    and Tuna with Castelvetrano Olives, 90, *91*
Energy Truffles, Dark Chocolate, *288, 289*

F
Fennel
    Lemon, and Dates, Braised Chicken Thighs with, 160,
        161
    -Lemon Ginger Tea, 228
Figs and Celery Root, Spatchcock Chicken with, 172–74, *173*
Flaxseeds
    Crispy Chicken Strips with Sweet and Spicy Mustard,
        163
    Easy Seeded Cracker Bark, 231, *234*
    Oatmeal Cookie Balls, *300, 301*
    Savory Granola with Thyme and Chile, 30, *31*
Fritters, Zucchini-Scallion Baked, *212, 213*

G
Garlic paste, preparing, 257
Gazpacho, Cucumber Melon, *130, 131*
Ginger
    -Carrot Dressing, 266, *269*
    -Carrot Shrimp Bowl, 175
    Gingersnap Granola Bars, 20, *21*
    Lemon-Fennel Tea, 228
    -Soy Turkey Meatballs with Miso Sweet Potato Noodles,
        147–48, *149*
    and Turmeric, Curried Tahini Dressing with, 266, 268
Granola, Savory, with Thyme and Chile, 30, *31*
Granola Bars, Gingersnap, 20, *21*

Grapes
    Pickled, 246
    Pickled, Scallions, and Celery, Lentils with, 70, 71
Green Beans and Teriyaki Chicken, Sheet-Pan, 136
Green Goddess Dressing, 271, 273
Greens. See also specific greens
    Fried Rice, Meaty, 204
    Power, Soup with Charred Scallions, 127
Gremolata, Parsley and Mint, 255

H
Halibut, Cilantro-Lime, Tacos with Crunchy Cabbage Slaw, 109
Harissa Sweet Potato and Squash Bake, 200, 201
Hazelnuts
    and Caramelized Onion, Cauliflower Rice with, 198
    Crunchy Dukkah, 256
    Scallions, and Dates, Roasted Cauliflower with, 214, 215
Herbed Yogurt Dip, 257
Herb(s). See also specific herbs
    Asparagus, and Leek Quiche, 42, 43
    Easy Veggie Pho with Coconut Broth, 124, 125–26
    Green Goddess Dressing, 271, 273
    Shrimp Summer Roll Lettuce Cups, 110, 111
    Tangy Ranch Dressing, 280
Horseradish Lemon Cream, Quick Vegetarian Borscht with, 128, 129
Hummus
    Beet, 237, 238
    Classic, 236, 237
    Green, 237, 239
    and Roasted Veggie Morning Bowl, 36

I
Ice Pops, Watermelon-Lime, 296, 297

J
Japanese Yam(s)
    Crispy Smashed, Barbecued Pulled Chicken on, 164, 165–66
    Cubes, Chili-Garlic, 220, 221
    Soy-Ginger Turkey Meatballs with Miso Sweet Potato Noodles, 147–48, 149
Juices
    Clean Up Your Act, with Apple, Celery, and Cucumber, 54, 55
    Emerald Eyes, with Fresh Greens and Mint, 58
    Pink, with Watermelon and Beet, 60, 61

K
Kale
    Cauliflower Tabbouleh, 82
    Chips, The Most Addictive, 230
    Emerald Eyes Juice with Fresh Greens and Mint, 58
    Kabocha Squash, Egg, and Quinoa Bowl, 18, 19
    Power Greens Soup with Charred Scallions, 127
    6-Minute Egg over Greens with Lemon-Anchovy Dressing, 34, 35

L
Lamb Chops with Cilantro-Peanut Chutney and White Beans, 176, 177
Leek, Asparagus, and Herb Quiche, 42, 43

Lemon
    Anchovy Dressing, 281
    Fennel, and Dates, Braised Chicken Thighs with, 160, 161
    -Fennel Ginger Tea, 228
    Red Onion, and Oregano, Branzino Stuffed with, 178, 179
Lentil(s)
    Black Bean Burger with Vegan Chipotle Aioli, 104–5
    Chicken Soup with, 121
    Dosa with Warm Dates, Yogurt, and Tahini, 308–12, 310–11
    with Pickled Grapes, Scallions, and Celery, 70, 71
    Red, and Carrot Soup, Lemony, 122, 123
Lettuce
    Cajun Salmon Burger, 114, 115
    Carrot-Ginger Shrimp Bowl, 175
    Cups, Shrimp Summer Roll, 110, 111
    Emerald Eyes Juice with Fresh Greens and Mint, 58
    Frisée with Delicata Squash and Green Goddess Dressing, 74, 75
    Grilled Chicken Paillard with Greek Salad, 84
    Lentils with Pickled Grapes, Scallions, and Celery, 70, 71
    Poblano Chopped Chicken Salad with Creamy Cilantro-Lime Dressing, 83
Lime
    -Cilantro Dressing, Creamy, 270, 271
    Miso Sauce, 260, 277
    -Watermelon Ice Pops, 296, 297

M
Mango
    and Citrus, Sliced, with Lime, Chile, and Smoked Sea Salt, 304
    Rainbow Collard Wraps with Crispy Tofu, 100–101, 102–3
Meatballs
    Bison, in Tomato Sauce, Sicilian-ish, 150–51
    Chipotle Chicken, Burrito Bowl, 152–53
Meatloaf, Feel-Good Turkey, 144–46, 145
Melon. See also Watermelon
    Baked Pears with Yogurt and Oats, 44, 45
    Cucumber Gazpacho, Creamy, 130, 131
    Melonballer Smoothie with Cantaloupe and Bee Pollen, 52
Millet and Roasted Broccoli Rabe with Cherries, 192, 193
Mint and Parsley Gremolata, 255
Miso
    -Glazed Sea Bass with Roasted Bok Choy, Sheet-Pan, 142, 143
    Lime Sauce, 260, 277
    Sweet Potato Noodles, Soy-Ginger Turkey Meatballs with, 147–48, 149
    Vegan Spaghetti Squash Carbonara with Mushroom Bacon, 168–69, 169
Muffins, Banana Pumpkin, 32, 33
Mushroom(s)
    Bacon, Vegan Spaghetti Squash Carbonara with, 168–69, 169
    Barbecue, Tacos with Tomatillo Salsa, 108
    Easy Veggie Pho with Coconut Broth, 124, 125–26
    Lightened-Up English Breakfast, 28, 29
Mustard, Sweet and Spicy, 251

N
Noodles
    Easy Veggie Pho with Coconut Broth, 124, 125–26
    Shrimp Summer Roll Lettuce Cups, 110, 111

Nori Popcorn, *226, 227*
Nut(s). *See also specific nuts*
    Milk, *62*
    Mix, Rosemary, Thyme, and Cinnamon, *224*
    soaking, *270*
    toasting, *199*

O

Oat(s)
    Affogato Oatmeal with Coffee and Coconut Cream, *27*
    and Almond Piecrust, *40–41*
    Blackberry and Plum Crumble, *298, 299*
    Blueberry Oatmeal Bake, *22, 23*
    flour, making your own, *17*
    Magic Pancakes with Bananas, Eggs, and Yogurt, *16, 17*
    Milk, *63*
    Oatmeal Cookie Balls, *300, 301*
    Savory Granola with Thyme and Chile, *30, 31*
    and Yogurt, Baked Pears with, *44, 45*
Oil, Chili Sesame, *252, 253*
Okra, Basil, and Snow Peas, Delivery Chicken with, *170, 171*
Olive(s)
    Castelvetrano, Endive and Tuna with, *90, 91*
    Faux Chickpea "Tuna" Salad, *78, 79*
    Grilled Chicken Paillard with Greek Salad, *84*
    Mixed, Tapenade, *225*
    Spatchcock Chicken with Figs and Celery Root, *172–74, 173*
Onion(s)
    Caramelized, and Hazelnuts, Cauliflower Rice with, *198*
    Quick-Pickled, *246, 247*
    Red, Lemon, and Oregano, Branzino Stuffed with, *178, 179*

P

Pancakes, Magic, with Bananas, Eggs, and Yogurt, *16, 17*
Papaya and Peach "Sorbet," *294, 295*
Parsley
    Cauliflower Tabbouleh, *82*
    Green Goddess Dressing, *271, 273*
    and Mint Gremolata, *255*
Parsnip(s)
    Chicken Soup with Lentils, *121*
    Soup, Creamy, with Manchego Crisps, *116–17, 119*
Pasta
    Bake, Roasted Butternut Squash, *162*
    Sunflower Seed Pesto, with Charred Zucchini, *138, 139*
Peach
    Grilled, and Radicchio Salad, *88, 89*
    and Papaya "Sorbet," *294, 295*
Peanut
    -Cilantro Chutney, *258, 271*
    Dressing, Crunchy, *274*
Peanut Butter
    Peanut-Chili Chicken Skewers, *188*
    and Pear, Power Up Smoothie with, *59*
Pear(s)
    Baked, with Yogurt and Oats, *44, 45*
    Emerald Eyes Juice with Fresh Greens and Mint, *58*
    and Peanut Butter, Power Up Smoothie with, *59*

Peas
    Asian Chopped Chicken Salad with Sweet Chili Soy Dressing, *86, 87*
    Meaty Greens Fried Rice, *204*
    Snow, Basil, and Okra, Delivery Chicken with, *170, 171*
Pecans
    Gingersnap Granola Bars, *20, 21*
    Savory Granola with Thyme and Chile, *30, 31*
    Sweet and Spicy, with Chipotle and Cumin, *222, 223*
Pepitas
    Coconut Chocolate Seed Clusters, *302, 303*
    Easy Seeded Cracker Bark, *231, 234*
    Gingersnap Granola Bars, *20, 21*
    Poblano Chopped Chicken Salad with Creamy Cilantro-Lime Dressing, *83*
Peppers
    Chipotle Chicken Meatball Burrito Bowl, *152–53*
    Hummus and Roasted Veggie Morning Bowl, *36*
    Poblano Chopped Chicken Salad with Creamy Cilantro-Lime Dressing, *83*
    Rainbow Collard Wraps with Crispy Tofu, *100–101, 102–3*
Pesto, Easy Sunflower Seed Cheeseless, *254*
Pho, Easy Veggie, with Coconut Broth, *124, 125–26*
Pickled Grapes, *246*
Pickled Onions, Quick, *246, 247*
Pico de Gallo, *249*
Pie, Red Berry Slab, *290–92, 291*
Piecrust, Oat and Almond, *40–41*
Pistachio(s)
    Crunchy Dukkah, *256*
    Dark Chocolate Energy Truffles, *288, 289*
Pizza, Roasted Tomato, with Quinoa Crust and Gremolata, *112, 113*
Plum and Blackberry Crumble, *298, 299*
Popcorn, Nori, *226, 227*
Pudding, Strawberries and Cream Chia Seed, *46, 47*
Pumpkin Banana Muffins, *32, 33*

Q

Quiche, Asparagus, Leek, and Herb, *42, 43*
Quinoa
    Blueberry Oatmeal Bake, *22, 23*
    Cauliflower Tabbouleh, *82*
    Chicken Soup with Lentils, *121*
    and Crispy Roasted Butternut Squash with Currant Vinaigrette, *210, 211*
    Crust and Gremolata, Roasted Tomato Pizza with, *112, 113*
    Kabocha Squash, and Egg Bowl, *18, 19*

R

Radicchio, Grilled, and Peach Salad, *88, 89*
Ranch Dressing, Tangy, *280*
Raspberry(ies)
    Baked Pears with Yogurt and Oats, *44, 45*
    Dark Chocolate Drops, *286, 287*
    Red Berry Slab Pie, *290–92, 291*
Rice
    Carrot-Ginger Shrimp Bowl, *175*
    Chipotle Chicken Meatball Burrito Bowl, *152–53*
    Dosa with Warm Dates, Yogurt, and Tahini, *308–12, 310–11*
    Forbidden, Coconut, *203*
    Meaty Greens Fried, *204*

Rosemary
    Italian Roasted Chickpeas, 232, 233
    Thyme, and Cinnamon Nut Mix, 224

S

Salads
    Asian Chopped Chicken, with Sweet Chili Soy Dressing,
        86, 87
    Cauliflower Tabbouleh, 82
    Corn, Cucumber, and Crab, Summer Market, 76, 77
    Egg, Middle Eastern, 68, 69
    Endive and Tuna with Castelvetrano Olives, 90, 91
    Faux Chickpea "Tuna," 78, 79
    Frisée with Delicata Squash and Green Goddess Dressing,
        74, 75
    Greek, Grilled Chicken Paillard with, 84
    Grilled Radicchio and Peach, 88, 89
    Lentils with Pickled Grapes, Scallions, and Celery, 70, 71
    Poblano Chopped Chicken, with Creamy Cilantro-Lime
        Dressing, 83
    Spinach and Crispy Tofu with Curried Tahini Dressing, 80,
        81
    Watercress with Apples and Manchego, 72, 73
Salmon
    Burger, Cajun, 114, 115
    Toast, Scandi-Style, 37, 39
Salsa
    Pico de Gallo, 249
    Verde (Easy Tomatillo Salsa), 245
Sauces
    Barbecue, 261
    Lime Miso, 260, 277
Sausages
    Lightened-Up English Breakfast, 28, 29
Scallion(s)
    Charred, Power Greens Soup with, 127
    Hazelnuts, and Dates, Roasted Cauliflower with, 214, 215
    Pickled Grapes, and Celery, Lentils with, 70, 71
    -Zucchini Baked Fritters, 212, 213
Sea Bass, Miso-Glazed, with Roasted Bok Choy, Sheet-Pan, 142,
    143
Seafood
    Branzino Stuffed with Red Onion, Lemon, and Oregano,
        178, 179
    Cajun Salmon Burger, 114, 115
    Carrot-Ginger Shrimp Bowl, 175
    Cilantro-Lime Halibut Tacos with Crunchy Cabbage Slaw,
        109
    Endive and Tuna with Castelvetrano Olives, 90, 91
    Lemon Anchovy Dressing, 281
    Scandi-Style Salmon Toast, 37, 39
    Sheet-Pan Miso-Glazed Sea Bass with Roasted Bok Choy,
        142, 143
    Shrimp Summer Roll Lettuce Cups, 110, 111
    Summer Market Corn, Cucumber, and Crab Salad,
        76, 77
Seed(s). See also specific seeds
    Clusters, Coconut Chocolate, 302, 303
    Easy Seeded Cracker Bark, 231, 234
    Nut Milk, 62
    toasting, 199

Sesame seeds
    Chili Sesame Oil, 252, 253
    Crunchy Dukkah, 256
    Easy Seeded Cracker Bark, 231, 234
    Nori Popcorn, 226, 227
Sesame-Soy Smashed Cucumbers, 208, 209
Shallot(s)
    Faux Chickpea "Tuna" Salad, 78, 79
    Vinaigrette, 280
Shrimp
    Bowl, Carrot-Ginger, 175
    Summer Roll Lettuce Cups, 110, 111
Smoothies
    Blue Seas, with Blueberry and Spirulina, 53
    Chai Turmeric, 56, 57
    Melonballer, with Cantaloupe and Bee Pollen, 52
    Power Up, with Pear and Peanut Butter, 59
"Sorbet," Peach and Papaya, 294, 295
Soups
    Chicken, with Lentils, 121
    Creamy Parsnip, with Manchego Crisps, 116–17, 119
    Cucumber Melon Gazpacho, 130, 131
    Easy Veggie Pho with Coconut Broth, 124, 125–26
    Lemony Red Lentil and Carrot, 122, 123
    Power Greens, with Charred Scallions, 127
    Quick Vegetarian Borscht with Lemon Horseradish Cream,
        128, 129
Soy-Ginger Turkey Meatballs with Miso Sweet Potato Noodles,
    147–48, 149
Soy-Sesame Smashed Cucumbers, 208, 209
Spices, grinding and toasting, 199
Spinach
    Blue Seas Smoothie with Blueberry and Spirulina, 53
    and Crispy Tofu with Curried Tahini Dressing, 80, 81
    Egg and Chutney Crepes, 96, 97
    Green Hummus, 237, 239
    Power Greens Soup with Charred Scallions, 127
    Power Up Smoothie with Pear and Peanut Butter, 59
    6-Minute Egg over Greens with Lemon-Anchovy Dressing,
        34, 35
Spirulina and Blueberry, Blue Seas Smoothie with, 53
Spreads
    Caper Aioli, 259
    Mixed Olive Tapenade, 225
    Sweet and Spicy Mustard, 251
    Vegan Chipotle Aioli, 250
Squash. See also Zucchini
    Banana Pumpkin Muffins, 32, 33
    Butternut, Crispy Roasted, and Quinoa with Currant
        Vinaigrette, 210, 211
    Delicata, and Green Goddess Dressing, Frisée with, 74, 75
    Hummus and Roasted Veggie Morning Bowl, 36
    Kabocha, Egg, and Quinoa Bowl, 18, 19
    Kabocha, Steamed Wedges with Lime Miso Sauce, 196, 197
    Roasted Butternut, Pasta Bake, 162
    Spaghetti, Carbonara with Mushroom Bacon, Vegan, 168–69,
        169
    and Sweet Potato Bake, Harissa, 200, 201
Strawberries
    and Cream Chia Seed Pudding, 46, 47
    Red Berry Slab Pie, 290–92, 291

Sunflower Seed(s)
    Cheeseless Pesto, Everyday, 254
    Coconut Chocolate Seed Clusters, 302, 303
    Creamy Cilantro-Lime Dressing, 270, 271
    Easy Seeded Cracker Bark, 231, 234
    Pesto Pasta with Charred Zucchini, 138, 139
    Savory Granola with Thyme and Chile, 30, 31
    Spinach and Crispy Tofu with Curried Tahini Dressing, 80, 81
Sweet Chili Soy Dressing, 275
Sweet Potato(es)
    Hidden Veggie Waffles, 25
    Miso Noodles, Soy-Ginger Turkey Meatballs with, 147–48, 149
    and Squash Bake, Harissa, 200, 201
Syrup, Date, 244

T
Tabbouleh, Cauliflower, 82
Tacos
    Barbecue Mushroom, with Tomatillo Salsa, 108
    Cilantro-Lime Halibut, with Crunchy Cabbage Slaw, 109
    Spicy Crunchy Cauliflower, with Ranch Slaw, 106, 107
Tahini
    Beet Hummus, 237, 238
    Classic Hummus, 236, 237
    Dressing, Curried, with Turmeric and Ginger, 266, 268
    Dressing, Simple, 266, 267
    Green Hummus, 237, 239
    Smoked Eggplant Dip, 234, 235
    Warm Dates, and Yogurt, Dosa with, 308–12, 310–11
Tapenade, Mixed Olive, 225
Tea, Lemon-Fennel Ginger, 228
Thyme
    and Chile, Savory Granola with, 30, 31
    Italian Roasted Chickpeas, 232, 233
    Rosemary, and Cinnamon Nut Mix, 224
Toast, Scandi-Style Salmon, 37, 39
Tofu
    Crispy, and Spinach with Curried Tahini Dressing, 80, 81
    Crispy, Rainbow Collard Wraps with, 100–101, 102–3
    Crispy, with Candied Brussels Sprouts, 156, 157
    Vegan Spaghetti Squash Carbonara with Mushroom Bacon, 168–69, 169
Tomatillo Salsa, Easy (Salsa Verde), 245
Tomato(es)
    Barbecue Sauce, 261
    Grilled Chicken Paillard with Greek Salad, 84
    Lightened-Up English Breakfast, 28, 29
    Pico de Gallo, 249
    Roasted, Pizza with Quinoa Crust and Gremolata, 112, 113
    Sauce, Sicilian-ish Bison Meatballs in, 150–51
    Sauce, Simple, Parm-less Eggplant with, 205–6, 207
    Spicy Slow-Cooker Chicken Chili with Black-Eyed Peas, 180–81

Tuna and Endive with Castelvetrano Olives, 90, 91
Turkey
    Meatballs, Soy-Ginger, with Miso Sweet Potato Noodles, 147–48, 149
    Meatloaf, Feel-Good, 144–46, 145
Turmeric
    Chai Smoothie, 56, 57
    and Ginger, Curried Tahini Dressing with, 266, 268
    Melonballer Smoothie with Cantaloupe and Bee Pollen, 52
Turnips and Carrots, Za'atar-Roasted, with Gremolata, 194, 195

V
Vinaigrettes
    Citrus, 277, 278
    Currant, 279
    Shallot, 280

W
Waffles, Hidden Veggie, 25
Walnuts
    Banana Pumpkin Muffins, 32, 33
    Braised Beets and Greens with, 190, 191
    Gingersnap Granola Bars, 20, 21
    Oatmeal Cookie Balls, 300, 301
    Savory Granola with Thyme and Chile, 30, 31
Watercress with Apples and Manchego, 72, 73
Watermelon
    and Beet, Pink Juice with, 60, 61
    -Lime Ice Pops, 296, 297
Wraps
    Chickpea Flour Crepe, 96, 98
    Collard Green Sandwich, 99
    Rainbow Collard, with Crispy Tofu, 100–101, 102–3

Y
Yams. See Japanese Yam(s)
Yogurt
    Bananas, and Eggs, Magic Pancakes with, 16, 17
    Chai Turmeric Smoothie, 56, 57
    Dip, Herbed, 257
    and Oats, Baked Pears with, 44, 45
    Quick Vegetarian Borscht with Lemon Horseradish Cream, 128, 129
    Red Berry Slab Pie, 290–92, 291
    Sheet-Pan Tandoori Chicken with Broccoli, 158, 159
    Tangy Ranch Dressing, 280
    Warm Dates, and Tahini, Dosa with, 308–12, 310–11

Z
Za'atar-Roasted Carrots and Turnips with Gremolata, 194, 195
Zucchini
    Charred, Sunflower Seed Pesto Pasta with, 138, 139
    Feel-Good Turkey Meatloaf, 144–46, 145
    -Scallion Baked Fritters, 212, 213

All photos by Amy Neunsinger except the following by Johnny Miller: i, iv-v, 3, 8, 30, 56, 61, 77, 89, 92-93, 130, 141, 157, 173, 177, 178, 182-183, 202, 211, 215, 226, 248, 252, 260, 262-263, 287, 297, 301, 307, 310-311, 317, 320

HarperCollins books may be purchased for educational, business, or sales promotional use. For information, please email the Special Markets Department at SPsales@harpercollins.com.

FIRST EDITION

DESIGNED BY RENATA DE OLIVEIRA

Library of Congress Cataloging-in-Publication Data has been applied for.

ISBN 978-0-06-242692-5

22 23 24 25 26   WOR   10 9 8 7 6 5 4 3 2 1